As Above, So Below

Heaven & Earth VI

Outdoor Art Exhibition
at Careek Park

July 12 - October 20, 2014

Sponsored by:

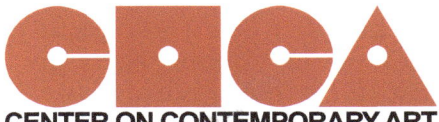

CENTER ON CONTEMPORARY ART

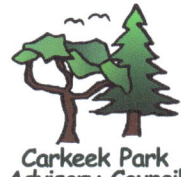

Carkeek Park
Advisory Council

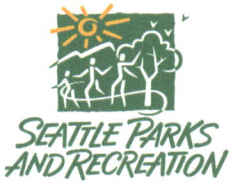

SEATTLE PARKS
AND RECREATION

Supported by:

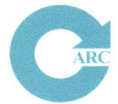

OFFICE OF ARTS & CULTURE

SEATTLE

CULTURE

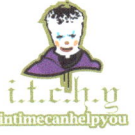

i.t.c.h.y
intimecanhelpyou

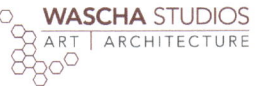

WASCHA STUDIOS
ART | ARCHITECTURE

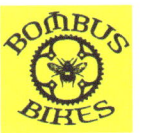

BOMBUS
BIKES

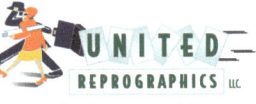

UNITED
REPROGRAPHICS LLC

www.unitedreprographics.com

Publisher

Support

CoCA

Published October, 2014 by:

CoCA
Center on Contemporary Art
5701 Sixth Avenue S., Suite 258
Seattle, Washington 98108

http://www.cocaseattle.org
info@cocaseattle.org
206 728-1980

Curator: Thendara Kida-Gee
Advisor: David Francis
Catalog: Ray C. Freeman III

Sponsored by:

Center on Contemporary Art
Carkeek Park Advisory Council
Seattle Parks and Recreation

With Support from:

4 Culture
Associated Recreational Council
Seattle Office of Arts & Culture
United Reprographics

Additional Thanks to:

i.t.c.h.y.
Wascha Studios
John at Renascence Trees
Friends of Llandover Woods
Tinker's Dram
Bill & Terry at Seattle City Light
Bombus Bikes
Paula Hoff
Belinda Chin
Tim Gee
David Francis
Ray C. Freeman III
Fred Lisiaus
Nichole DeMent
Stephen Rock
David Koon

Contents

35 Years of Creative Passion

Nichole DeMent

CoCA's passion for the spirit of individuality in art is going on 35 years old. We are a longstanding icon in Seattle that's worked with thousands of artists including Chuck Close, Laurie Anderson, Annie Sprinkle, Joel Peter Witkin, James Turrell, and Nirvana to name a few. When CoCA Curator and then Vice President, David Francis, ideated Heaven & Earth at Carkeek Park six years ago, he essentially ignited the passion of nearly 100 contemporary artists, hundreds of volunteers and 50,000+ *annual* visitors in a mutual spirit of imagination and innovation.

This spark also brought together a non-profit arts organization; a passionate group of neighbors, community members and volunteers who support and enjoy Carkeek Park; as well as the City of Seattle's Parks and Recreation Department for an unprecedented collaboration which continues to provide creative opportunities for artists in a beautiful urban park.

The Center on Contemporary Art's mission is to serve the Pacific Northwest as a catalyst and forum for the advancement, development, and understanding of Contemporary Art. Heaven and Earth's continued growth and support from its surrounding community and visitors from afar, as well as ongoing support by diverse organizational partners solidly establishes CoCA's mission and passion for contemporary art is a healthy counterpart to Seattle's spirit of individuality. I am continually humbled by what so few can accomplish with so little and humbly thank the hard work of this year's curator, Thendara Kida-Gee, all of the sponsors, volunteers, as well as the CoCA board and interns that made this exhibition happen. Most of all I thank the artists that turn the world upside down and inspire us to slow down and think about things in new ways.

Nichole DeMent
President, 2014
Center on Contemporary Art

Above and Beyond

Foreword

David Francis

In selecting "As Above, So Below" as this year's theme for the *Heaven and Earth* exhibition series, curator Thendara Kida-Gee reconnects us with the metaphysical connotation that initially defined the artwork in 2009. This ancient maxim, identified with the pagan prophet Hermes Trismegistus (second century BCE), echoes again and again throughout Renaissance and Enlightenment scholarly texts that seek the underlying secrets of the natural world. Isaac Newton, for instance, like many early scientists, was familiar with the phrase and referred to it in his many writings, most of which remain unpublished. The sense of a grand interconnectedness (*vernetzung*) that links one world to another remains more important than ever in our time, as Seattle again experienced record-breaking heat, the second hottest summer on record after the year 2000 (79.3 average temperature).

Curating an art exhibition in a forested 216-acre (87.1 ha) public park visited by tens of thousands of people who are apparently underexposed to art is not an easy task. Every year the unsecured sculptures are not only touched, but so thoroughly "used" that some become more ephemeral than lasting. Perhaps this too is in keeping with the original intent that in an ideal case scenario, there would be nothing to remove in the end. While each of the artworks is a physical object in the park, there is a vast component to their structure that does not emerge until time passes. In essence, the way that time interacts almost arbitrarily, affecting different pieces in different ways, is part of the art. The sum total of each piece consists of matter, natural weathering, and cultural interaction. The artworks are catalysts for the imagination and serve a vital role in a late Capitalist society otherwise obsessed with celebrity, consumption, and pleasure.

Having participated as an artist in 2011 and 2013 (with her husband Tim Gee), Thendara knew full well what risks were involved. Even so, my initial estimate of 100+ hours to curate the show was way off and the actual total is closer to five times that amount. Unable to provide much help from my temporary home in Hong Kong, I worried about how things were going on the other side of the world. At the Hong Kong Museum of Art, I took the kids to see a concurrent exhibition called "Heaven, Earth, and Man" occupying the outdoor plaza along Kowloon's waterfront. Everyhere you looked, there were small shrines with incense smoking and an offering of fruit. It seemed as though there really was a link.

In the end, "As Above, So Below" became the strongest version of the show yet, with a new record for submissions, new partners and collaborators, 11 (of 16) new artists, and a revitalized commitment that has re-inspired my previously flagging energies. Thendara and Tim have not just done an amazing job of curating one of the most challenging exhibitions in the Northwest, they've reinvented it, reaching new audiences (Elder Wise, Groundswell NW, Parent Map, La Raza NW, etc.). As the ancient hermetic text indicates, it's not just that "above" and "below" share this mystical connection, it's "the miracle of the One Thing" that binds them together, the telos, the ineffable essential that resists (or escapes) the artist's intention.

From 2009 – 2014, over 50 artists have exhibited in Carkeek Park. Upwards of $100,000 (grant money and income from the Carkeek Park Advisory Council's partnership with Associated Recreation Council's summer day-camp program Earthkeepers) has been devoted to the ongoing exploration of art, nature, and the human experience. With MadArt now established…and NePo 5k walk, LoFi on Smoke Farm, the city's ArtsParks and Sidewalks programs – is there a need for this exhibition, given the damage? Has it been shelved in the art commu-

David Francis, PhD

nity's mind as "uneven" (Arts writers Michael Upchurch, Brian Miller, Jen Graves all use this term)? Anyone with a regional eye on the scene or a hunch about what's going on internationally knows the answer – that's why every year artists from across the country, internationally even, apply every year. Maybe we'll never get Andy, Anish, Agnes, or Mark or Bob to come on down and give *Heaven and Earth* a shot, but with the regional and national interest that Thendara has inspired, it's clear that the potential is there for the kind of artist that still takes risks and experiments with possibilities, that recognizes the value of non-commercial work, and the increasing importance of igniting collective imagination in an otherwise impoverished, tele-vised mass-culture of easily-digestible entertainment.

Thendara's efforts to make the exhibition more accessible, as she explains in her statement, created three main areas for investigation. As soon as the jetlag had faded a bit after my return, I went to the park, beginning with the lower meadow and returning several times to walk as far as the upper meadow and playfield and its hidden grove, the knoll beside Picnic Shelter #2. On each visit, I delighted in NOT being the curator at last, in being a simple denizen of the park for the first time in six years. And yet I couldn't resist that impulse, the caretaking gesture that I observed in others, the replacing of parts, the replacing of signage, the uprighting of the fallen. In a sense, this exhibition turns the community into a community of caretakers or curators, stewards of the fragile artworks that in turn summon the metaphysical connection to the natural world's own precariousness. My eternal gratitude to Thendara and Tim, to CPAC, CoCA, and Seattle Parks, and to this remote corner of the country where, surrounded by an embarrassment of riches in terms of broadly similar eco-art exhibitions and interventions in environments we thought we knew, *Heaven and Earth* remains strikingly unique, idiosyncratic and challenging, a place where perhaps the wildest trials of all may find a home among the trees and trails. In a time when our interpretations of 'wilderness' are now openly contested (as the heavy-handed control of photography by the US Forest Service recently underscored), it's a necessity that art keep ahead, that it strive to keep hinting at the possibilities.

David Francis, PhD
Curator, 2009 - 2013
Advisor, 2014
CoCA Board Member, 2005 -

Notes from the Curator

Thendara Kida-Gee

To illuminate the title a bit more, consider the words attributed to Hermes Trismegistus a few thousand years ago: 'That which is below is like that which is above, and that which is above is like that which is below, to accomplish the miracles of One Thing'." These hieroglyphic characters were carved into an emerald tablet around 1900 BC. This seemingly innocuous statement has had a profound influence on philosophers, alchemists, theologists and scientists throughout the ages, and ever since, interpretations abound.

For my purpose, and in my mind, *As Above so Below* describes both the duality that dominates our lives and thinking (mind and body, life and death, heaven and earth, male and female, physical and spiritual) with a deeply mystical understanding that whilst we hold these dualities to be opposites, they are in fact reflections of each other, the same but different, one created from the other. An example would be, an artist inspired to create a sculpture (above, mental) builds it out of stone and metal (below, physical). Through the artist the Above became the Below, through making thoughts real, the artist expresses the higher ethereal feeling and emotions into something solid and tangible.

It also points to a two-way process, a mutual dependence with each side feeding the other's existence, as the tree branches stretch to reach the sun, as its roots dig deeper to tap the water. Though the roots are hidden from our sight, we have all seen images of how they reflect the growth of the branches above. Looking at nature in this way, and seeing that the roots are dependent on the branches and leaves, and the leaves dependent on the root, neither dominate, both nourish and sustain the life of the One Thing (the Tree). Such is the delicate balance and interchange between the above and the below; the process is ageless and somehow unbreakable, the balance exquisitely fragile.

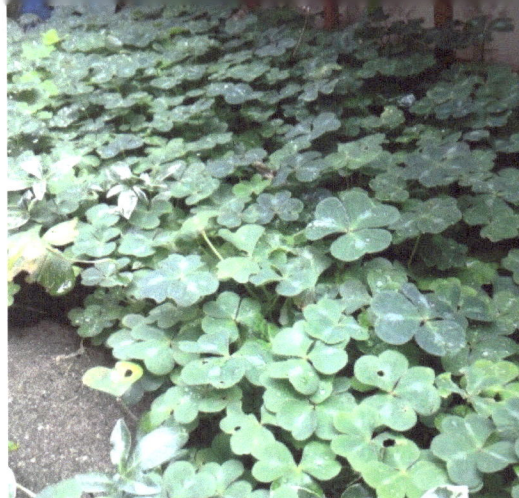

Oxalis, from Meredith Hall & Vaughn Bell's 'Post Colony' at Heaven and Earth 2009

I first met *Heaven and Earth* back in 2009. I had just moved in up the road and never heard of Carkeek Park much less its infant art exhibition prior to stumbling in on opening day. We adopted a plant from the artists Meredith Hall & Vaughn Bell whose piece 'Post Colony' included formal adoption of native plants, and who kindly allowed us to take on an *Oxalis*, which has since taken over my small city garden in the same way *Heaven and Earth* took over my heart, for its trusted exuberance of both art and nature.

Five years later David Francis (Curator of *Heaven and Earth I - V*), invited me to take over the helm. This is an exhibition that is more of a pot luck vs a host-and-guest situation. There are so many fingers in the pudding it would amaze you and it is all built on relationships reaching from community arts to local government and a lot of spaces in between. It proves how much can happen with so many supporters

and I for one are grateful for its birth and presence in our North Seattle Community which is not as blessed as our South Seattle cousins to have such a bountiful art scene. I was absolutely honored to be asked to be a part of this exhibition which I watched from birth through toddler-hood and beyond.

I understood from experience that for the artist there is a huge amount of faith and positive perseverance that goes into exhibiting in a public park, to work on something to set it free with the potential that it might never be seen the same way again. And then there is nature - which can lend a hand to all sort of mischief. I wanted to work with such an intrepid crew and the journey didn't disappoint.

Learning from previous years

We wanted to address accessibility, for everyone (artists as well as audience). One of my favorite aspects of the exhibits in previous

years was the mystery trail of works, the surprises in the woods, but these isolated pieces were often missed by those of limited mobility who weren't able to make it to the higher steeper trails and their surrounds.

The arrangement proposed this year was to create three galleries, each serviceable by a parking area at their edge. A person with limited mobility might get driven to the locations and be able to move between pieces, vs taking the longer, full park hike. It brought pieces into the open as well in hopes that being this blatant, we might elicit the public to help keep watch and foster park-goers as docents and defenders of the art. It was an unabashed stepping out from the woods and into the daylight - a loss of mystery but also a little easier to share with everyone vs just those in the fittest condition. Our call to artists was free, giving access to artists from far and wide & varying economic levels. We additionally welcomed the public to join us, to meet the artists during installation week, furthering the position of viewer as shareholder of this public display.

Our signage also encouraged a more out-in-the open sharing of information. As the mystery trail of 2009 -- 2013 turned into gallery spaces in 2014, we also identified artworks with artists and information about the piece.

This year artists created bold works. Some of the accepted proposals were recognized as being risky, easily damaged and targeted for shenanigans. How much trust can we give people and is it suspiciousness that leads to mischievousness?

A World Wildlife Report last month offered the grim statistics that populations of mammals, birds, reptiles, amphibians and fish have declined by an average of 52% over the last 40 years. Is it right for everything human to live long and always prosper or do we need to confront this decay,

this delicacy on display to show audiences that life is fragile?

These choices, we believe, helped in the ways we intended. This year's show has suffered minimal interference, thankfully none malicious. Some works designed to weather weathered well, others built to withstand nature withstood.

The Artists

This year's menagerie was introduced to the park at the beginning of July 2014. Sixteen artists installed their work, initiating their direct relationship with the park, and its inhabitants. The week of installation became a baptism of sun and heat for our crew and as we had just passed solstice; the light stayed late. Sun burns and dehydration became part of the struggle to raise art. Some of the pieces were meant to survive the long, three-month haul, being sturdy and unyielding, while others were more fragile. Each served as a bridge to bring art folks into

nature and nature folks to some art and all varying unsuspecting sorts of picnickers, ball players, kite flyers and wanderers to mention a few, in a setting away from the harsh lights and white walls of a commercial gallery.

Gallery 1 - ELC

Enter the Park - to the Environmental Learning center - where we visit four pieces;
two of which monuments made to weather and two are ephemeral experiences made to wither.

Suzanne Tidwell's 'Meadow Aloft' beckons first from over the shrubs in the parking area, brightly coloured flower tops showcased in the summer sun. As their season passed they experienced falling stems from over-exuberant interactions that left them at times worse for wear. They jingle with the right amount of shake which is a gentle shake not a forceful pull to and fro; but how do you reiterate this to the public? Even when the flowers came down it just took a different life form - the autumnal version very apparent by September, mimicking my own garden's rise and eventual inevitable downfall.

After opening weekend, Mother nature and her dry heat completely turned Mary Coss's 'DNA Planta Genetica', DNA pods (woven around a standing dead tree) into a fallen nurse log. Nature offered transformation unexpectedly, initially causing frustration, but eventually embodying a change that all grew to appreciate. The tree fell in a tidy manner, not even knocking the signs down and not breaking her piece at all -- just becoming encompassed in the DNA pods in a captive fashion and also on the ground vs in any upright tree-like fashion. The danger of a dry snag. Parks allowed us to keep it as it was, an example of transformation (with additional help from the artist) as the season matured.

Steady as she goes: in between these two more mobile and easily

harassed pieces sit sculptures by Lucy Mae Martin and Kristin Schimik. Both served as bird perches, feeding areas and have had bird-made additions throughout the summer. Kristin's 'Spiral Set' moves into and above the earth or above and into the earth, standing strong and unflinching, stained in warm berry tones.

Lucy Mae's 'Elements of Life' stone circle welcomes a place for man or bird to explore tactilely as well as visually. The closer one gets, the more desire there is to touch the symbols of nature and the heavens, blasted into stone, welcoming the fingers' exploration as well as providing an inviting resting place.

Gallery 2 - Lower Meadow

In the lower meadow gallery, we have pieces that focused our gaze inwards and through in some cases, exploring the inner space of the art or the outer space of the art as a filter to the world. Allyce Wood offers us contrast

from the green of the moss and trees with her safety-orange symbols of protection gently hanging from the row of trees as you first hit the lower meadow in her piece 'Periapt'. The orange from a distance resembles graffiti but only as an illusion as this piece as well as the others are created under the desire that at the end of this show there is no harm done and no trace or remnant that remains; it was just a moment and it will not be marked into permanency.

From Minnesota, Elisa Fonseca's 'Stalagmites' sit under a tree reaching towards the branches as it roots surface from beneath the tree, 'as above so below.' As the season progressed they went from colourful pieces outside of nature practicing some bio mimcry, to a more hidden presentation by October when the colors became muted under the mud; they now resembled something eerie, something escaping from below.

Michael Harrison's 'Sanctuary'

offered a place to gaze inwards, perfectly nestled amongst some fir trees, a magical space we have all experienced at some point; a sanctuary, a space where time stands still and moments can be frozen into symbols of remembrance enhanced by fragile objects contained inside. A porch to walk up enticed folks to peep through its mossy cracks, see what's inside, a memory? a moment in suspension?

Meagan Treasure offers us another inversion in her 'Earthly Obscura' which sits in a circle of trees flipping the world on its head with a camera obscura encapsulated in reclaimed clay. Tom Hughes works with materials intended to devolve, creating with cardboard. Tom presents a devolution as his piece was squashed in the first two weeks - rekindled to two new pieces commemorating the first Glider which had the temporal beauty of a large insect with a textual message " We Belong Everywhere." Dianna Pindell's 'Willow Water'

offered us an appreciation for a tree's drip line, how its extension beneath the earth's surface mimics the branches above. Prior to exhibition, we nearly lost this Willow tree completely, due to rot. After a massive hair cut (trim), potentially the tree equivalent of a bowl cut, the tree stood firm, less willowy & more army, but it survived -- allowing Deanna's mosaic of reflections to capture from below what hangs above.

Joshua Harker came to us from Chicago and crafted 'Crania Geodesica'. His installation week was long and his journey not an easy one. Twigs were gathered from the park and other local parks and cut to size; 522 pieces individually labeled for precise arrangement, each with eyelets installed. A frame was made to winch the skull up into a state of suspension whilst being built - when complete it would be gently lowered to the lawn. Joshua soon realized how different working with founds sticks vs purchased doweling rods was: he suffered hand pains for

weeks after installation. Mid-season the Crania collapsed, remaining slightly concave for the Autumn.

Gallery 3 - Upper Playfield

In the upper playfield, which becomes the busiest of areas in the park, we hosted playful pieces exploring movement, sound, and reflection.

Fred Lisaius' 'Slow Dance' resembles a barren puzzle of a tree suspended from its underside, swaying gently in the wind, reflecting its once-owned rootball that would have spread below. Teresa Burrelsman-Stern played with reflections of the trees above in her parabolic mirrored bowl entitled 'Sky Feeder', made from 281 mirrors and dowels; it was one of the most delicate pieces that sustained throughout.

Terra Holcomb created a chandelier composed of moss and woodlands elements ranging between two snags like a forest jewel, offering potential play & habitation to the local squirrels, birds and insects, giving the dead trees a helping hand with ornamentation. Ken Turner's 'Projections and Reflections on the Moment' would reflect, then merge the sky with the land with the sea, offering itself as a beacon or standing sentry, following the wind, or anyone tall enough to spin its highly reflective mylar mirrors. Savina Mason uses the wind to inhabit the ears of those lucky enough to pass at just the right time: aluminum nails dancing in their suspension affixed to the 'Sound Tree'. Sound Tree became another favorite perch for the crows and their fledglings as summer set in.

3 months, countless visitors later

As September headed into October and the sun faded a bit earlier we saw works surviving - some having weathered the race well; other pieces ran the race but defiantly suffered its length.

Finishing installation for an art show often offers a de-crescendo moment, one where all work ceases and things are left up to the work to, well, work. This exhibition has a lifecycle that sees no de-crescendo in sight, all flux and sway, but hopefully enough creative momentum to keep it going long into the future.

Thank you to Martin Carter who created our visual presence for *As Above, So Below*.

Thank you to all the artists. Thank you to everyone who helped make *Heaven and Earth VI* a reality.

Thendara Kida-Gee
Curator, 2014
Participating Artist 2011, 2013
CoCA Board Member, 2013-2014

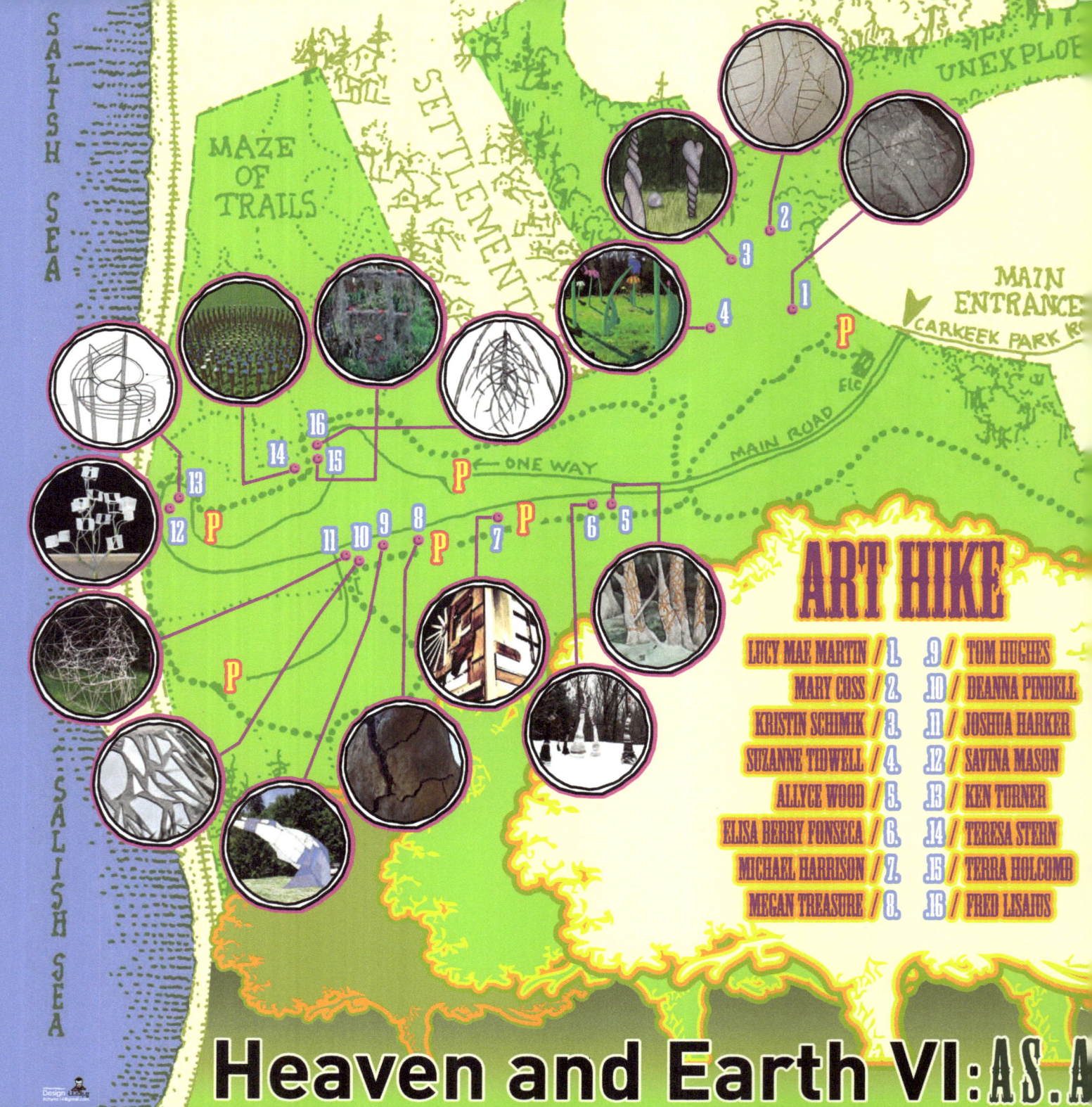

Heaven and Earth VI: AS.A

SALISH SEA

SALISH SEA

MAZE OF TRAILS

SETTLEMENT

UNEXPLORE

MAIN ENTRANCE

CARKEEK PARK RO

ELC

MAIN ROAD

ONE WAY

ART HIKE

LUCY MAE MARTIN / 1.	.9 /	TOM HUGHES
MARY COSS / 2.	.10 /	DEANNA PINDELL
KRISTIN SCHIMIK / 3.	.11 /	JOSHUA HARKER
SUZANNE TIDWELL / 4.	.12 /	SAVINA MASON
ALLYCE WOOD / 5.	.13 /	KEN TURNER
ELISA BERRY FONSECA / 6.	.14 /	TERESA STERN
MICHAEL HARRISON / 7.	.15 /	TERRA HOLCOMB
MEGAN TREASURE / 8.	.16 /	FRED LISAIUS

Design

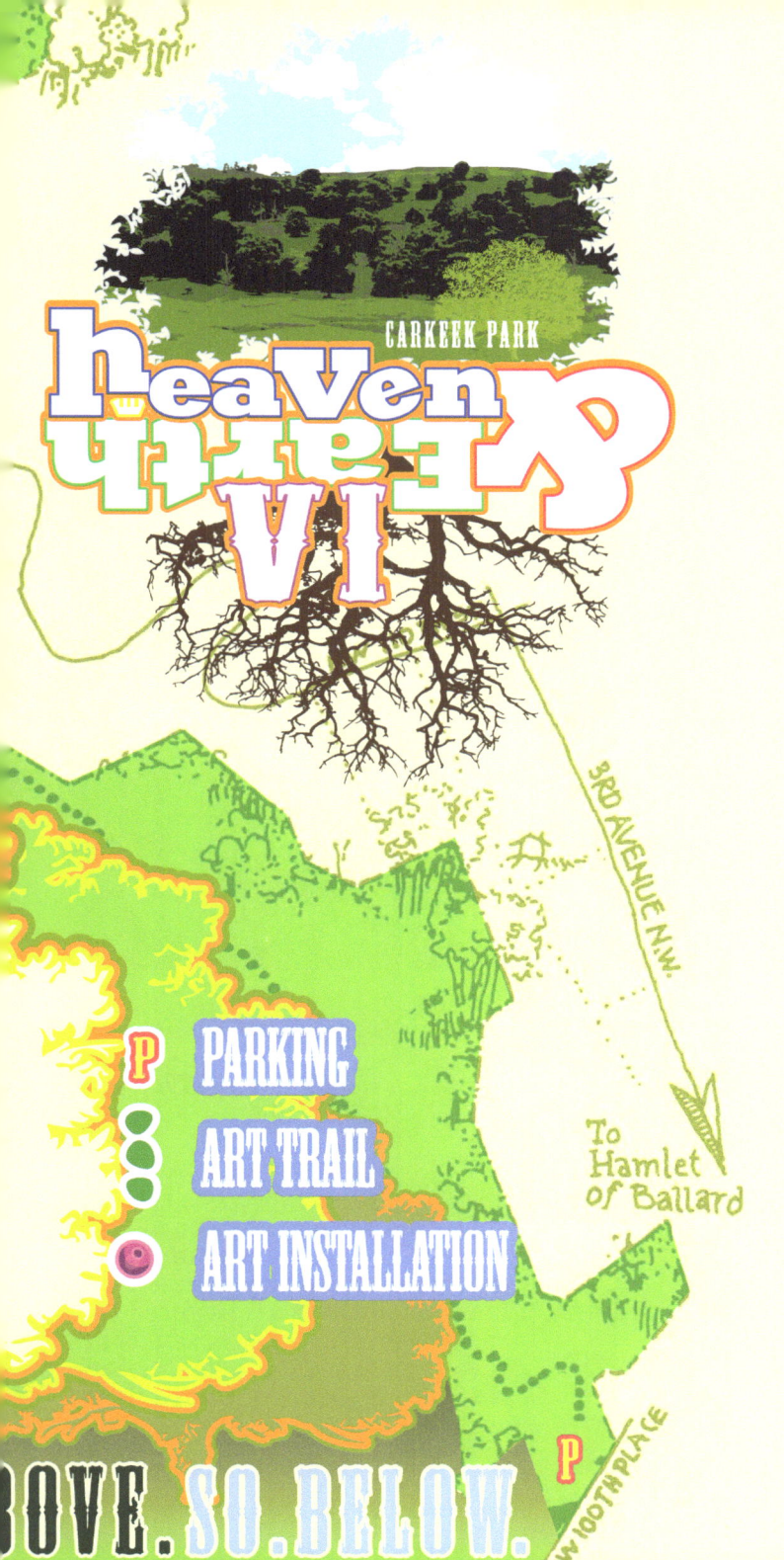

Art Hike Map

The numbers on the following pages refer to the locations on this Art Hike Map, created by Martin Carter over an original drawing by Ray C. Freeman III, which was in turn based on the CPAC Trail Map, a sketch by David Francis, and A. A. Milne's map of the 100 Acre Wood.

Over 1,200 maps, donated by United Reprographics, were given away to visitors during the course of the show.

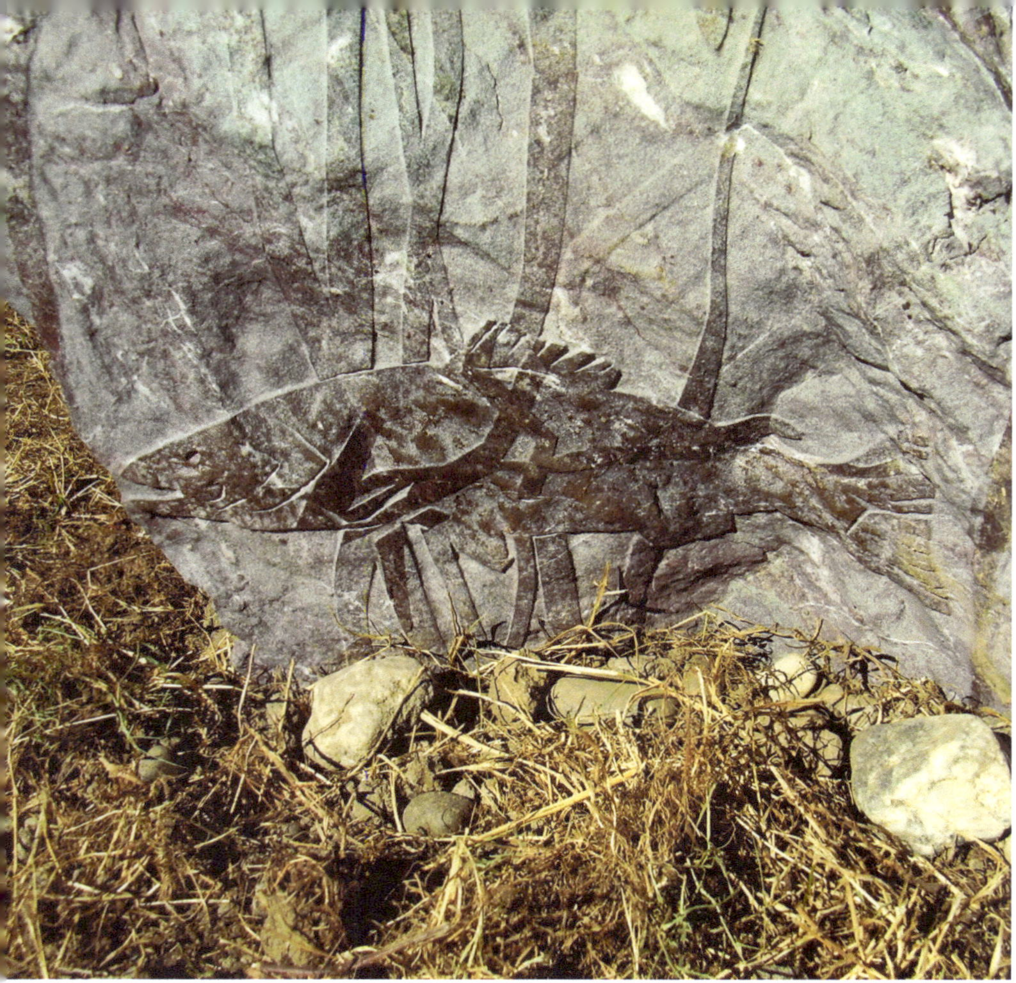

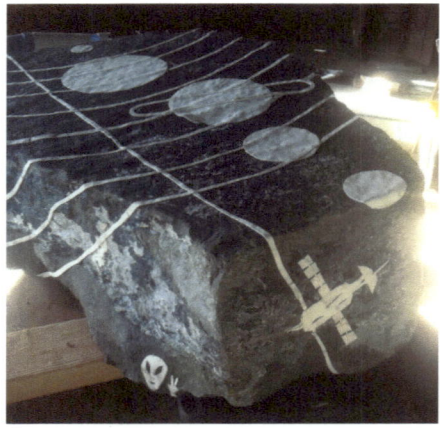

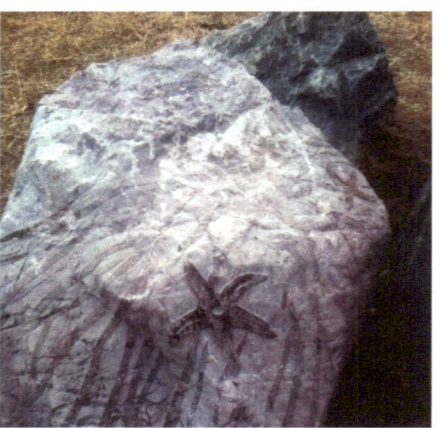

"Heaven is under our feet as well as over our heads."
-Henry David Thoreau

These 3 stones represent the skies, the waters, and the idea that art can be touched and enjoyed by everybody in their own individual way. I am inspired to sandblast relief style because it reveals thousands of years tucked away inside each beautiful, unique rock.

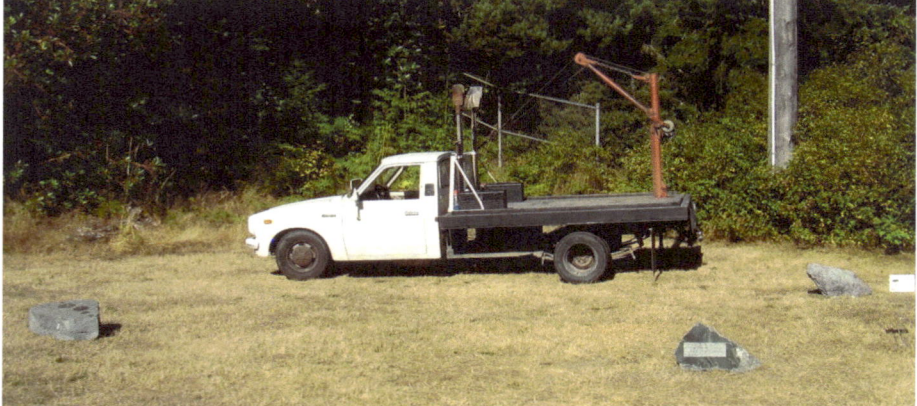

Lucy Mae Martin   http://www.toddsmonuments.com

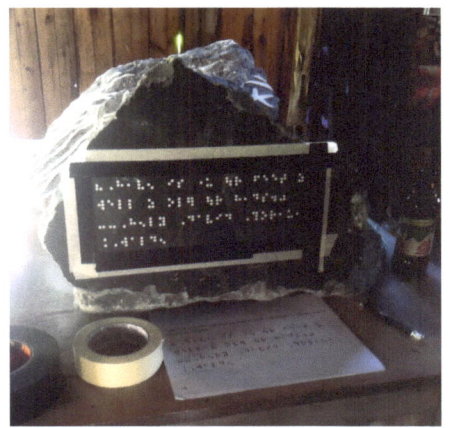

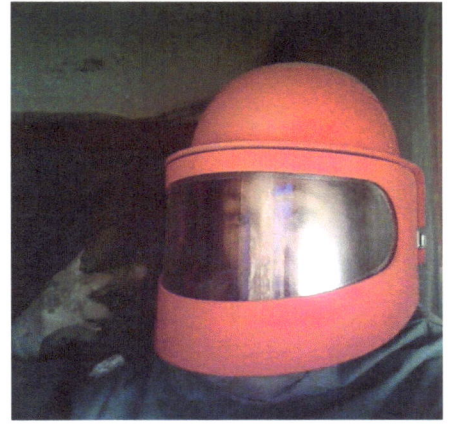

1

Elements of Life

Lucy Mae Martin

Martin's studio is an old barn along the slough in Conway, WA that her dad helped set up, equipped with a wood burning stove and a beautiful view of the foothills on the east, and the Olympics in the far west. The studio serves two purposes; a headstone business her father owned until 2007, when he generously offered the business to Lucy, and two; her art studio.

Lucy Mae Martin grew up on the Fir Island flats of Skagit Valley, WA. She learned at an early age to work with her hands, and has a deep appreciation for oddities, connecting with people, and adventure.

These wrapped and sandblasted stones represent a lighter side of my heavy, creative work life. I am inspired to engrave relief-style because there are millions of years tucked behind the surface of every beautiful, unique stone and the sandblasting reveals these layers.

The engraved Braille stones are a direct reflection of my thought that everyone should be able to enjoy art in their own individual way~

I had an amazing opportunity to meet (and will continue working side by side) with a large group of low vision and blind artists in Seattle, Vision Loss Connections to find out, 'what is it that you would like to see again?' and wow, what a response: a boat in the water, a quail, a skeleton, a deciduous tree, maple leaf, the Space Needle, an octopus, it was an incredible moment to hear all of this! And then to be able to engrave some of these images and put their Braille title in stone!!!

So incredible! The first Braille stone I made was a rock that I engraved r-o-c-k Braille characters into, I decided to see if my humor was just as funny to somebody who reads or is learning Braille....

Once the woman realized that the C and the K were not an M and a B, there was a smile and laughter to follow.
She actually read my Braille rock. And laughed :)

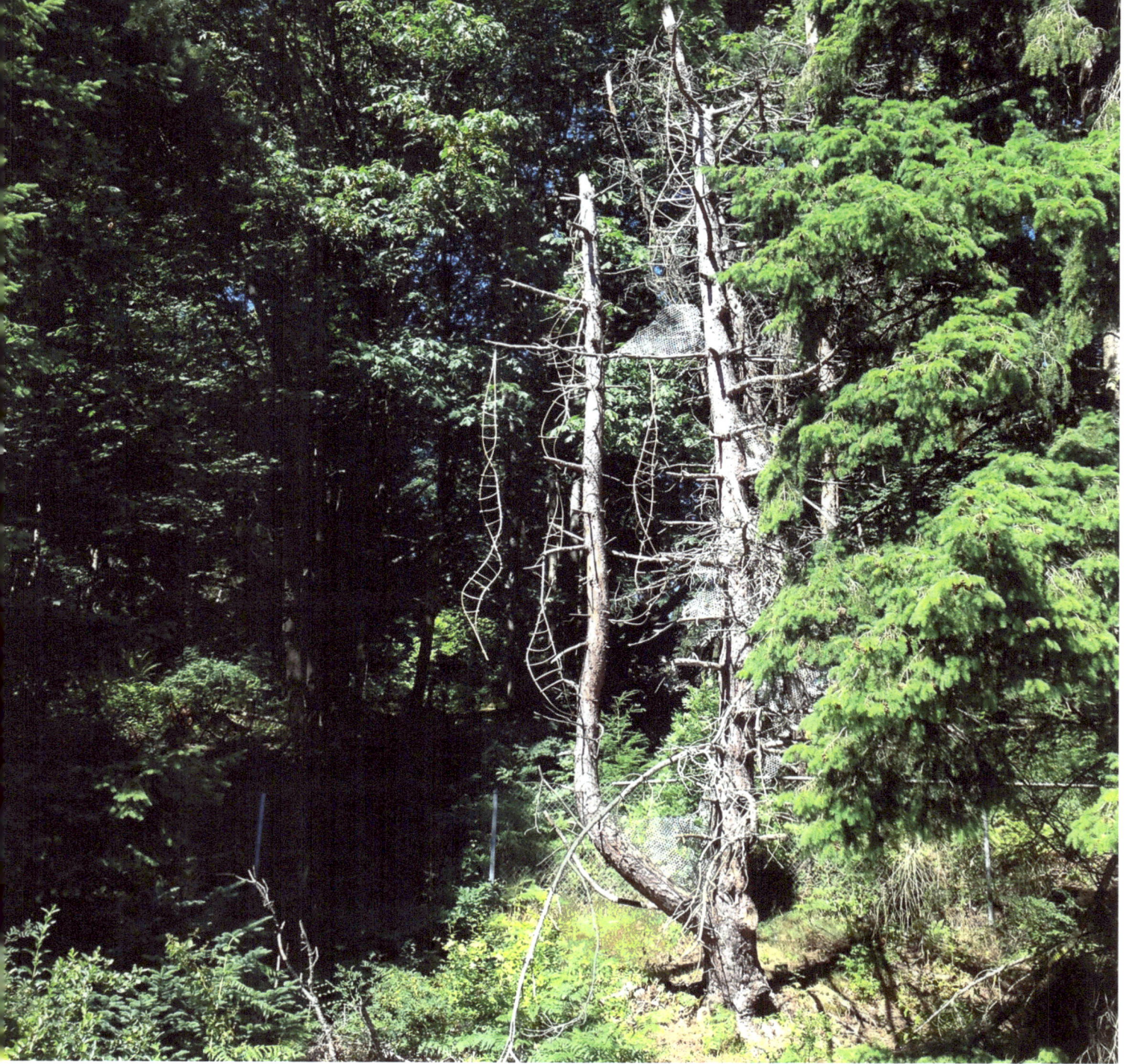

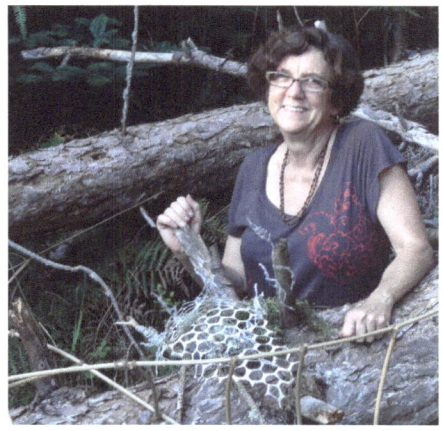

2

DNA
Planta Genetica

Mary Coss

Mary Coss received her Master of Fine Arts from Syracuse University and has accumulated an extensive exhibition record, focusing on alternative venues and community and public art projects. Coss has received residencies and grants from institutions including the Candyland Arts Center in Stockholm, the James and Janie Washington Foundation, 4Culture, the National Endowment for the Arts, San Juan Island Museum and Sculpture Park, and Seattle's Office of Arts and Culture.

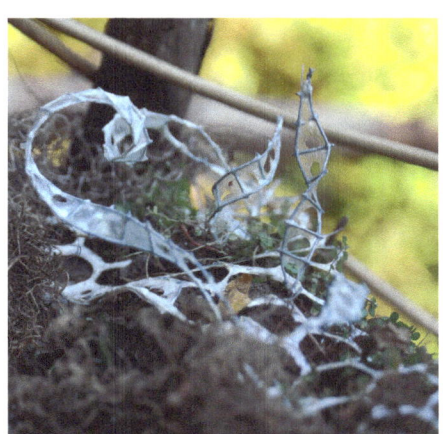

"If a tree falls in a forest and no one is around to hear it, does it make a sound?"

I am interested in the intersection of nature and the human made. Melding imagery from genetics with the forest opens a conversation to explore issues of the sacred, the discrepancies between the sanctity of life and progress in science. Installing art within the natural world brings a unique perspective to the conversation.

I walked into Carkeek Park to find a location for my DNA pods and was halted in my tracks by the powerful presence of a once vibrant fir tree. The looming carcass spoke to me and to the work. The ladder like limbs rose 30' tall and echoed the form of the DNA pods, suggesting an unfurled double helix. It seemed the perfect site to question our relationship with nature, and the consequences of intervention.

Ironically, with the help of City Light and a piece of heavy equipment, a mechanized boom lift I was able to hang my light and fragile 5 pounds of pods and

webs throughout the tree without impacting the tree in a significant way. Opening weekend I marveled as the helix pods spun in the wind in a mesmerizing hypnotic way I hadn't anticipated, picking up light as the dappled sunlight moved across the forest in endless transformation.

Call it irony, nature's satire, or paradox, the morning light revealed the tree had fallen. Remarkably the DNA pods were nearly unharmed, intertwined throughout the fallen form. The forest was speaking to us.

A conversion occurred and a DNA nurselog was born. It seems the smallest micro DNA has blossomed. Certain living matters can take up the DNA of the surrounding environment in a natural occurring phenomenon called transformation. It occurs when the "bacteria" is competent. I'm not truly a scientist, but I believe the pods were competent and transformation has started.

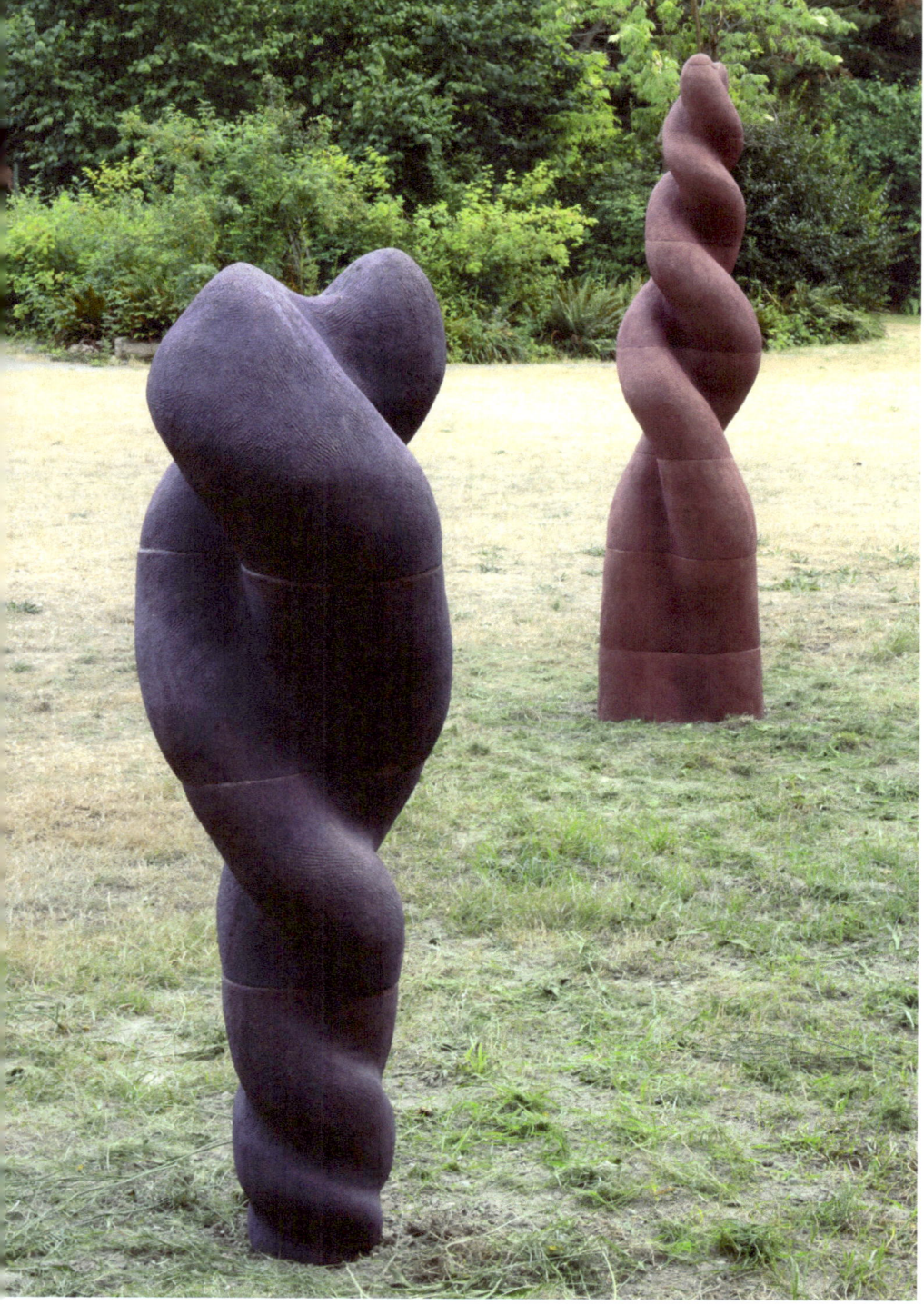

Art making, for me, is a visual and spatial act to honor the overlooked. Good art has heart. The heart serves to integrate a fragmented consciousness.

My work takes many forms: sculpture, objects, installation, and public projects that respond to a given site. Of interest in all cases is the question of value. How can I honor what is overlooked and often discarded?

Creation occurs in a state of reverence and appreciation for my surroundings. Through focusing my hands and body in the ritual and repetition of art making, the process and the tangible outcome becomes a deeper gesture of gratitude and awareness.

Kristin Schimik   http://kristin-schimik.weebly.com

3

Spiral Set

Kristin Schimik

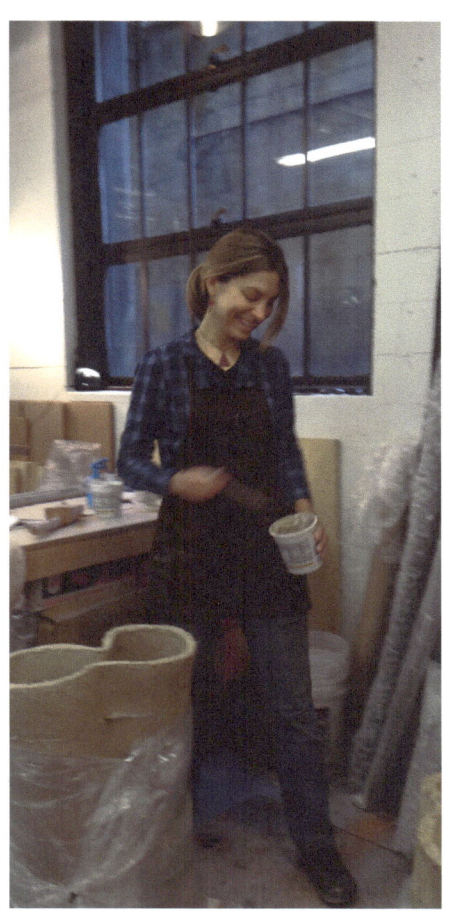

Kristin Schimik is a sculptor originally from Michigan, who lives and works in Seattle, Washington. Recent exhibitions include JUNCTURE: New Sculpture, in January 2014, and A Meditation for Carbon, in March 2013, at The Gallery at Pottery Northwest, Seattle. Schimik was awarded a grant from 4Culture SiteSpecific in 2013 for The Infinity Loop Project, an installation sculpture and performance at the historic Renton Mine Hoist Foundation in Washington State. Her work has been included in the 2012 Taiwan Ceramics Biennale in Taipei, Taiwan and Alchemy: From Dust to Form at the Harn Museum of Art, Florida. Schimik holds a BFA in Sculpture from Northern Michigan University and was awarded a Graduate Fellowship from the University of Florida while earning her MFA in Ceramic Sculpture in 2010.

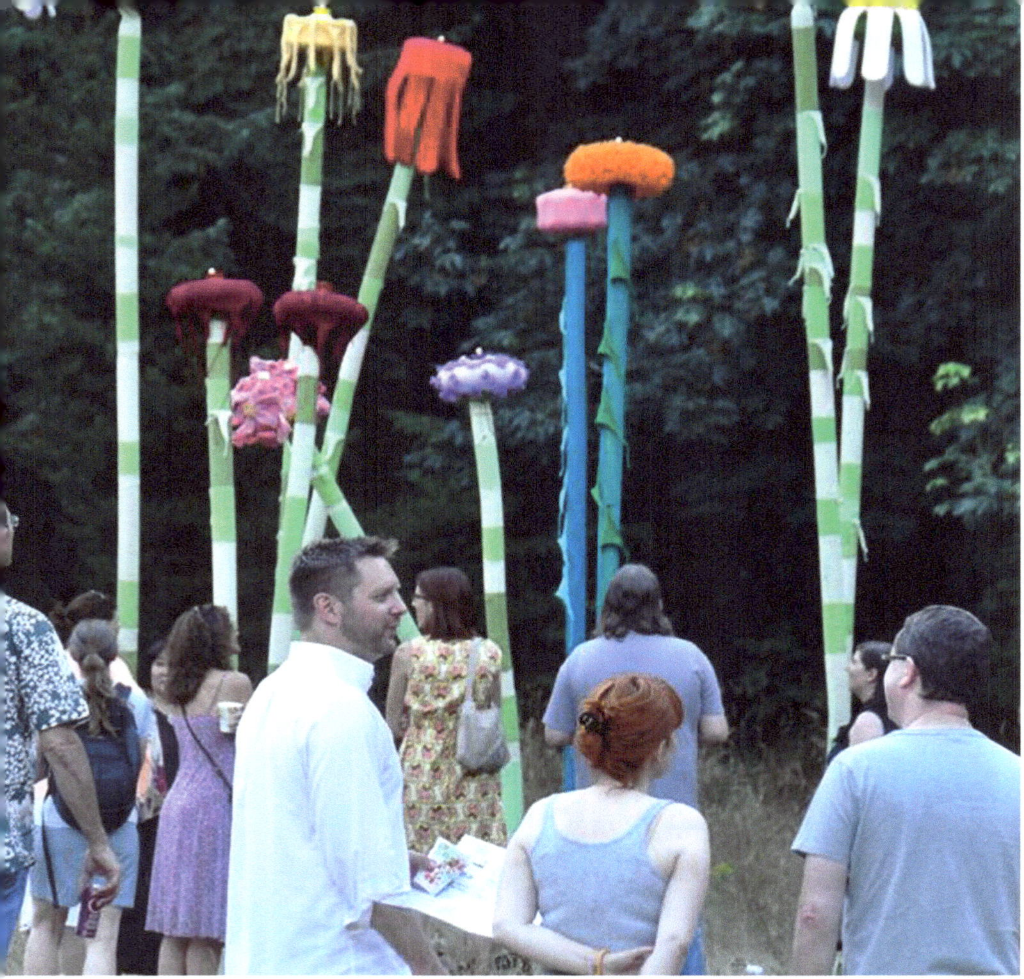

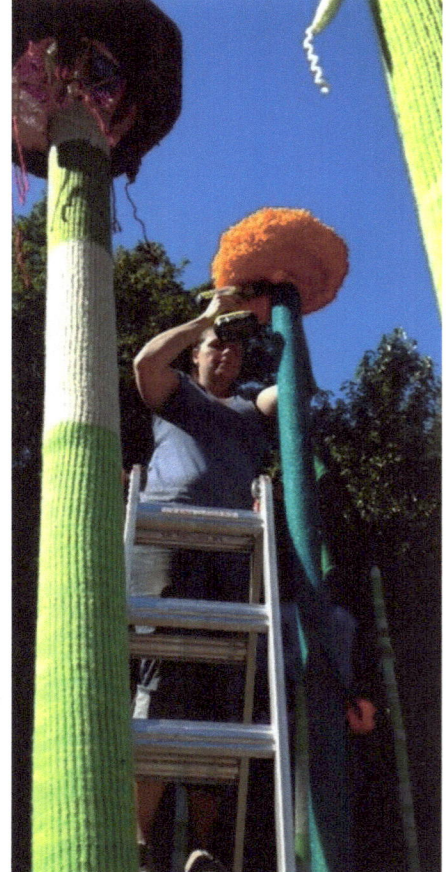

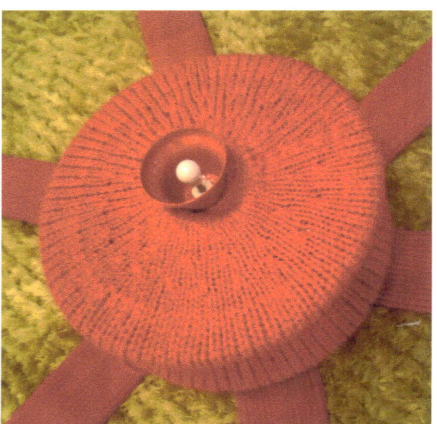

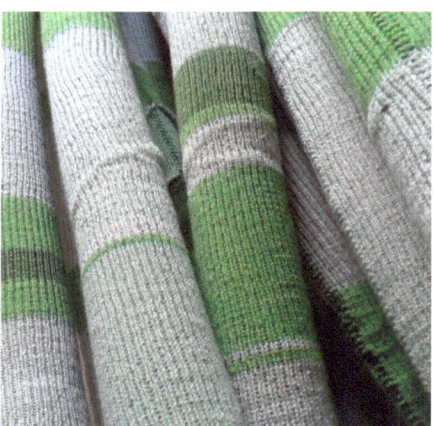

4

Meadows Aloft

Suzanne Tidwell

My goal as an artist is to encourage people to live in the moment and enjoy the color and beauty of their environment. Even if it's rainy and overcast, we can always find something joyful to admire. We spend so much time getting from one place to another. We often don't stop to appreciate what we are passing. People often ask me why I display my work outside. I want to encourage people to get out of their cars and into public parks and spaces. My whimsical stripes make people smile. We can certainly use more smiles in our day.

A city's desirability is measured by its ratio of developed areas to green spaces. The irony is while everyone likes the idea of their city having lots of parks, very few people use them. My installations increase attendance in local parks, drawing people in with bright color, taking visitors by surprise and compelling them to enter the space. What's most amazing is these visitors take pictures and share images of my installation with friends over social media, influencing their friends to visit the park…and so on…and so on. It warms my heart to see spaces I've transformed full of people. That's how I measure the success of my projects.

Why Fiber? I think fiber sort of found me. I've always been interested in the history and tradition of making things by hand. I find comfort in the feel of the materials, joy from bright color, and satisfaction with the repetition. Creating with fiber is how I respond to the world around me. It's my history and my present. I can't speak to the future just yet, but for now, I'm happy to just keep knitting…who knows what will inspire me next.

Meadow Aloft is a sensory field of 30 giant blooms atop 10-15 foot stems. By means of gentle hand or casual breeze, chimes of different tones will ring as the flower heads sway back and forth. Miles of brightly colored yarn recycled from past projects have been re-knit to form the petals, stems, and leaves of the entire project.

When hiking and walking, people rarely look up, unless sound directs them. Most prefer to gaze ahead or down below, carefully watching their footing. Color, texture, sound, and movement join forces to beckon hikers from nearby trails toward this bright, soaring garden. My installation will offer an alternative view from which we usually observe native flora, offering immersion in a sea of cheerful color and the somewhat rare opportunity reach out and actually touch the art. "Leave nothing but footprints, take nothing but pictures, kill nothing but time."

Sponsored in part by 4Culture. With special thanks to Greg Bartol for his invaluable help securing and storing materials, welding expertise and understanding when five really means fifty.

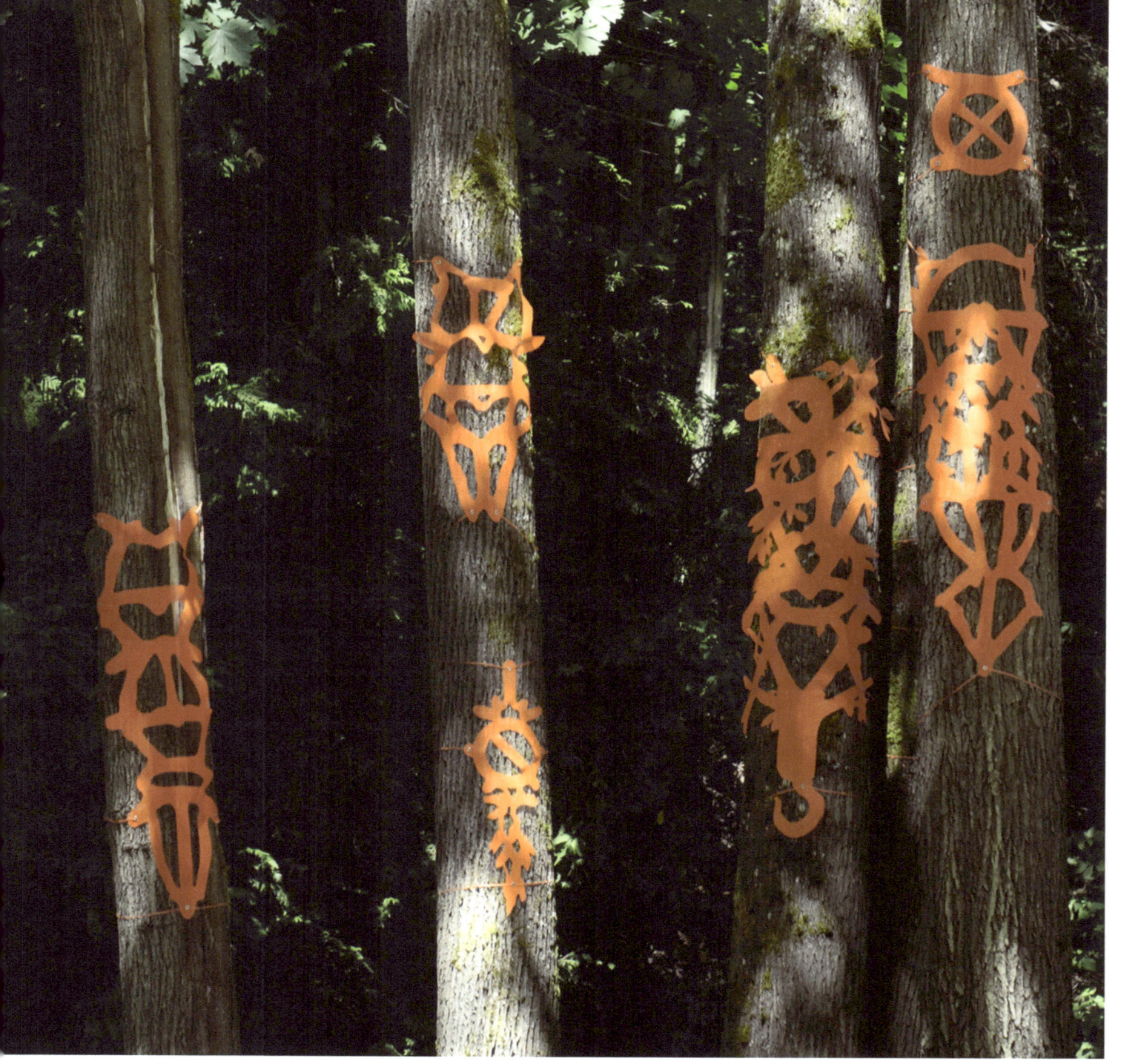

Allyce Wood

Allyce Wood is based in Seattle and a graduate of Cornish College of the Arts (magna cum laude) 2010 with a BFA in printmaking and sculpture. She studied Environmental Sculpture at Glasgow School of Art in 2009. Wood has been a member of SOIL Artist Run Gallery since 2012. Her work has been shown in cities such as Glasgow, Oslo, Oakland, *New York, and Seattle.*

Wood's work focuses on ecological consequences of industry and human interaction. Her aesthetically complex installations, drawings, and prints, mindfully illustrate humanity's negative influence on the natural world and the subsequent longterm consequences.

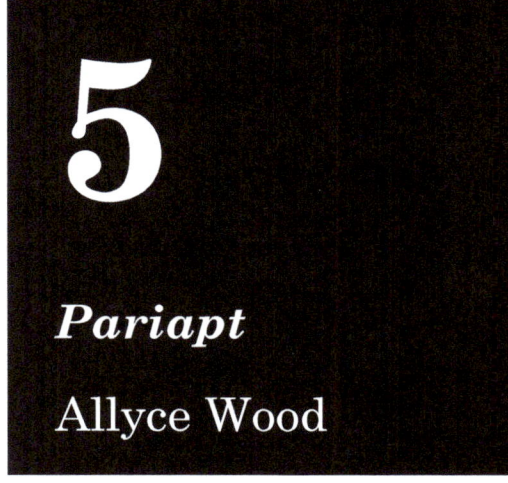

5

Pariapt

Allyce Wood

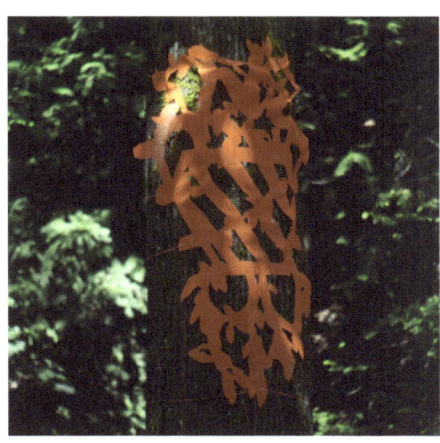

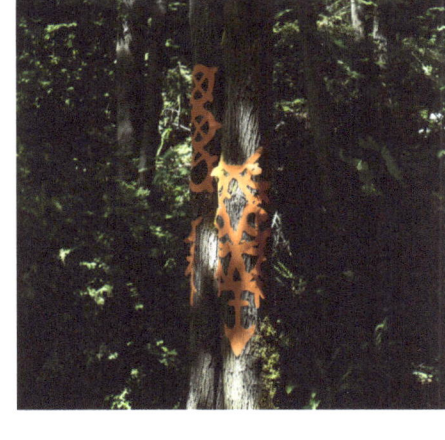

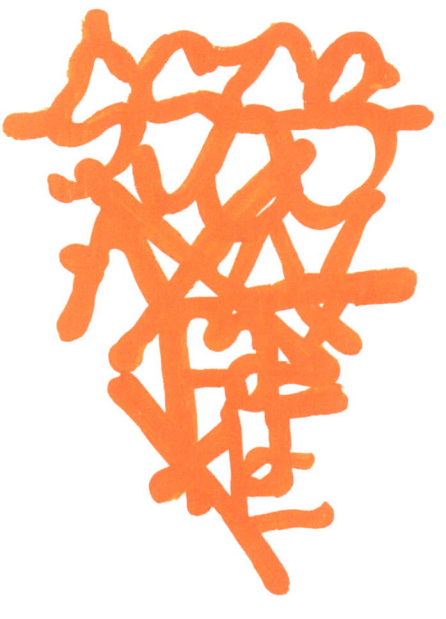

'Periapt' refers to an amulet worn for protection, in this case, the implied preservation is granted to trees through a bright orange installation. An immediate symbol for environmentalism, trees act as a typical cause for ecological awareness. Their de facto earthly purpose, symbolism, and anthropomorphism makes for strong emotional links. In incorporating them into this work, they are enmeshed in new symbology of construction materials, second skins, and safety. They are demarcated as 'priority' specimens, alluding to conservationists common actions to protect certain species and territories. The installation is composed of elements based on industrial signage, artistic gestures, and the 'Protect This Tree' flyers seen in downtown construction areas. By pairing such loaded medium with evocative symbology, humanity's inescapable duality as protector/destroyer is brought into sharp focus.

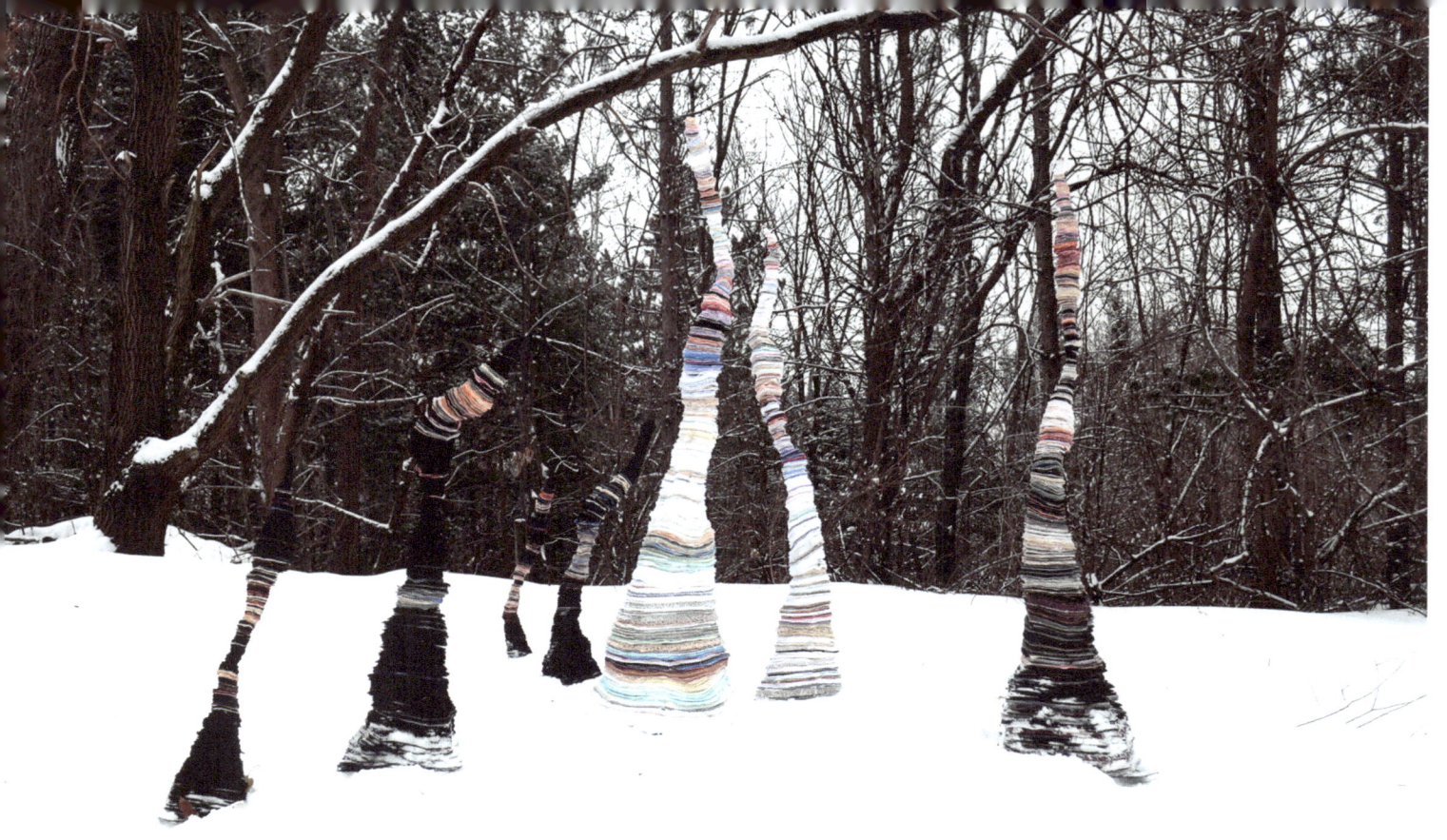

We import meaning to the landscape, all the while believing that meaning comes not from ourselves but from the landscape outside of ourselves. Even in a representation based on observation, such as a photograph, the artist's mind is visible in the framing of the shot, affirming that, "in landscape painting only subjective representation is possible, since landscape has only a reality in the eyes of the beholder" (F. W. J. Schelling). Human craft is a response to a desire to unify nature and reveal its hidden personality.

With that in mind, I perform repetitive actions on particular media in order to imitate nature's processes and forms. Cut and stacked tarpaper, fabric and felt accumulate into twisted, contorted stalagmites climbing out of the floor. Veins of single layers of material insert subtle lines. Such a process of production is analogous to the way that sediment draws stripes on rocks and canyons. Only in this case, my own hand fabricates the fantastical landscape and the playful creatures that inhabit the space of art.

Elisa Fonseca

http://www.ebfonseca.com

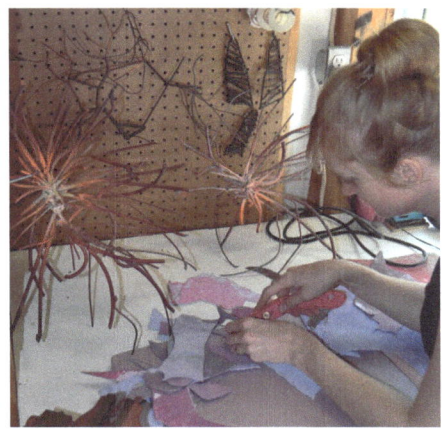

6

Stalagmites

Elisa Fonseca

Elisa Berry Fonseca completed an MFA in Sculpture from the University of Minnesota in May 2012. She holds a Master of Arts in Religion and Art from Yale Divinity School and a BA from Macalester College.

She has exhibited her work extensively and has enjoyed a number of opportunities to give lectures about the intersection of art criticism, art history, aesthetics and theology. Elisa was a 2013 recipient of a grant from the Minnesota State Arts Board. Along with making and talking about art she enjoys teaching, writing, building communities and being outdoors. Currently Elisa lives in Minnesota with her husband.

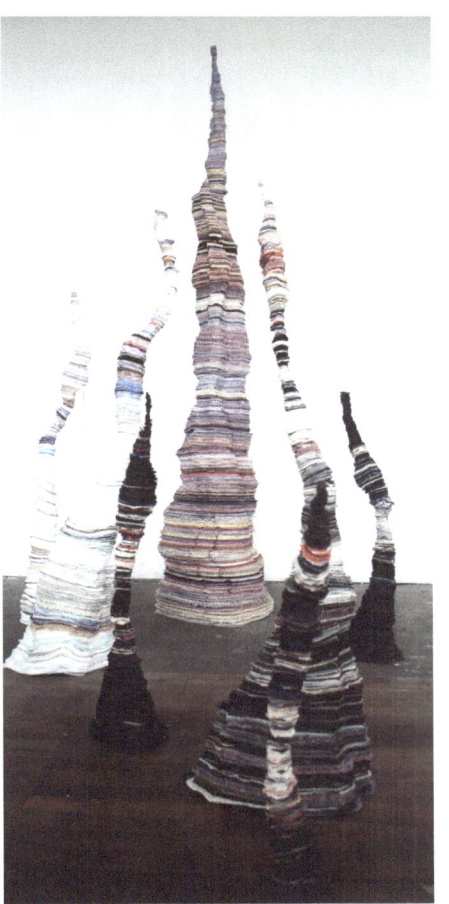

The experience of the work changes at different distances. Up close, viewers want to investigate the material specificity of the work, as well as the way that it is made. Zooming out presents a picture of a strange and fantastical landscape.

These varying levels of encounter allow viewers to shift between different ways of receiving information, from eye to hand to body. Since the work references nature but also human action, it considers the role of human beings in the construction of nature.

The stalagmites are made primarily of tarpaper, plywood, and fabric treated with roofing compound, so as to withstand the elements.

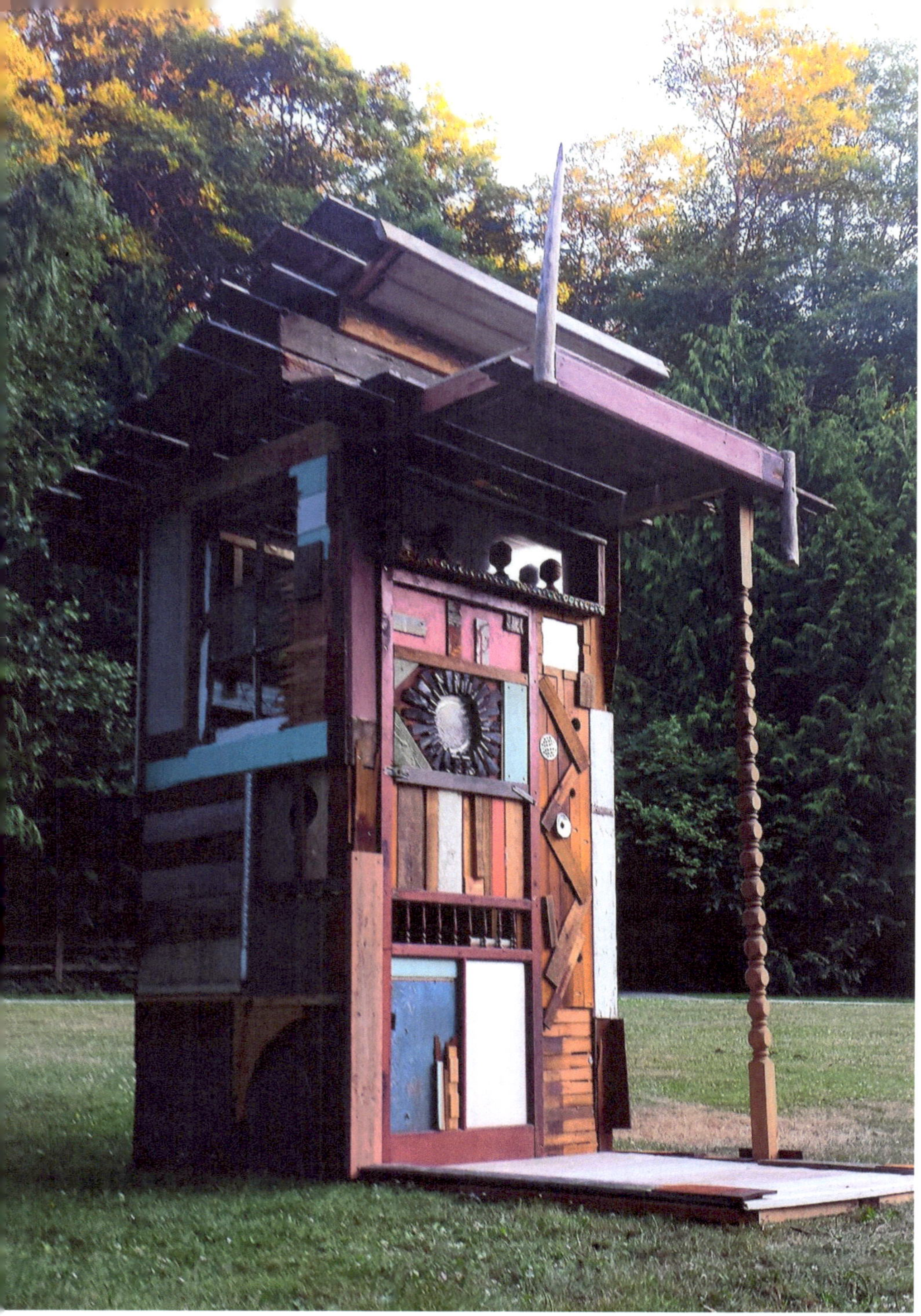

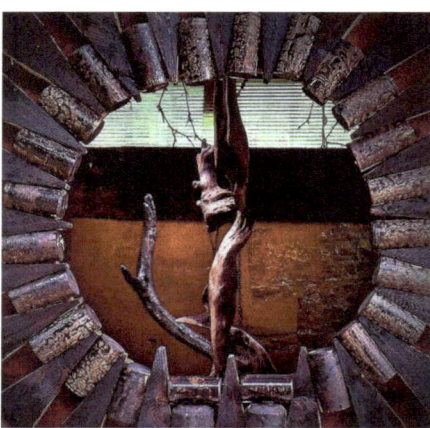

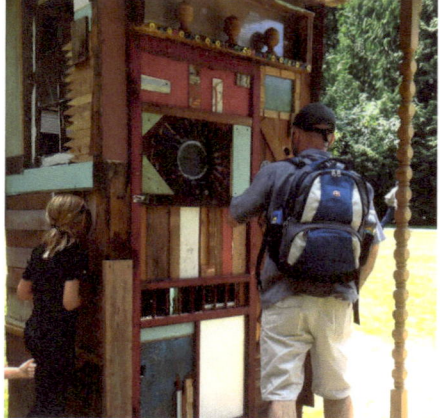

Michael Harrison   http://www.michaeltoddharrison.com

Sanc·tu·ar·y

: a place where someone or something is protected or given shelter
: the protection that is provided by a safe place
: the room inside a church, synagogue, etc., where religious services are held

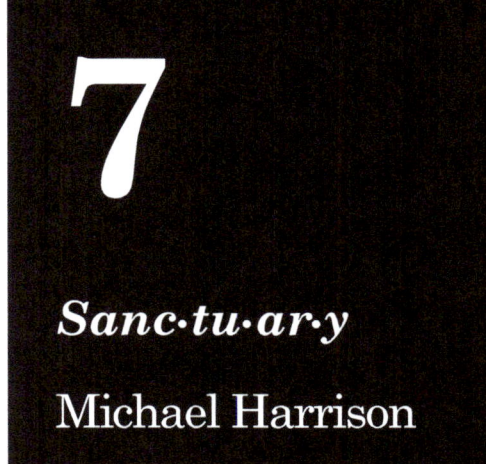

7

Sanc·tu·ar·y

Michael Harrison

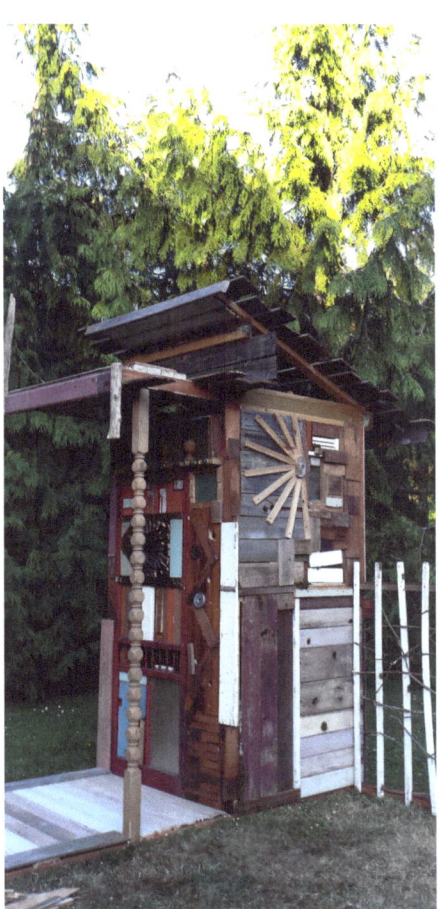

We all in our own way seek shelter, acceptance and security. As technology marches forward - offering the illusion of excitement, inclusion and connectedness with the world around us - we become more and more isolated. We lose touch with our surroundings. Instead of experiencing the Grand Canyon, a U2 concert, Puget Sound, we take phone pics. We text, we Tweet, we Facebook the experience, but do we really SEE it, EXPERIENCE it?

"Sanctuary" represents this dichotomy and invites the viewer into rich, glowing inaccessible place. It also invites the viewer to look through the piece - beyond the perceived safety of isolation - to see once again the incredibly beautiful natural world. It is only in nature that true sanctuary exists.

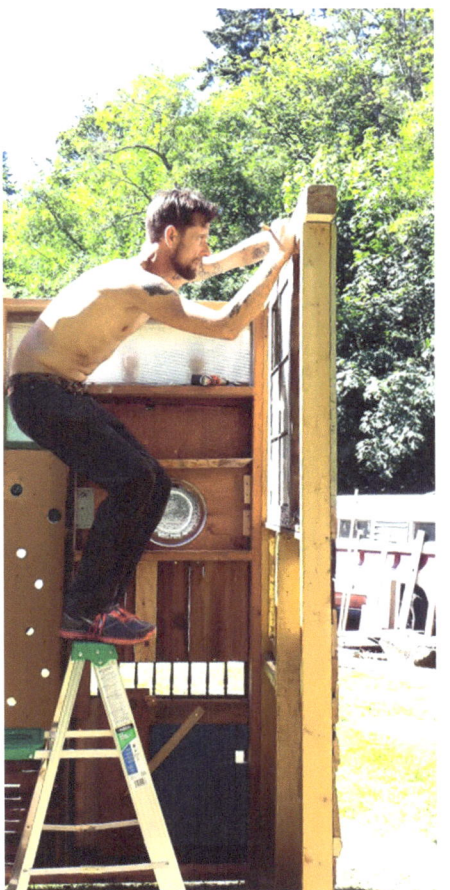

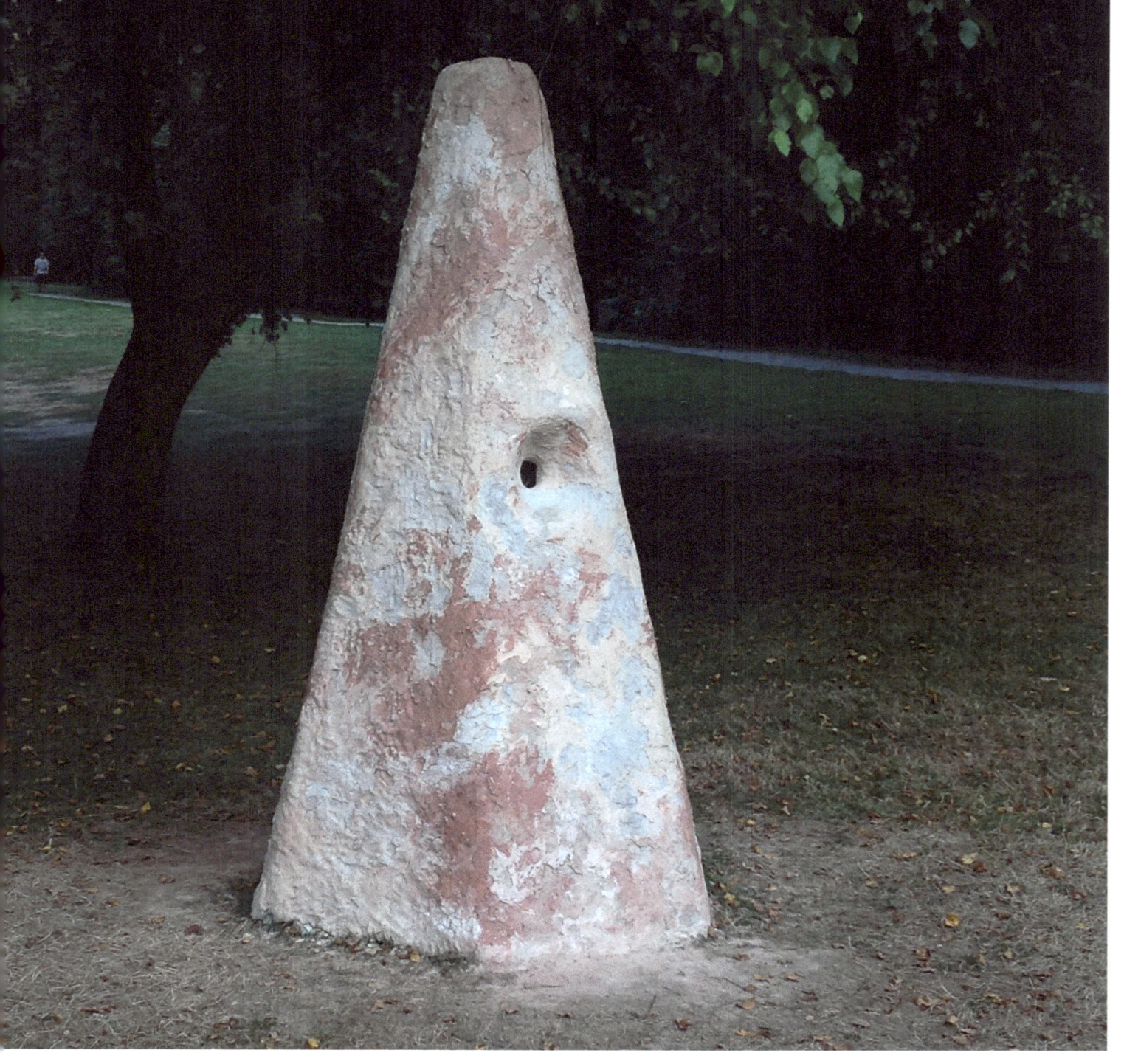

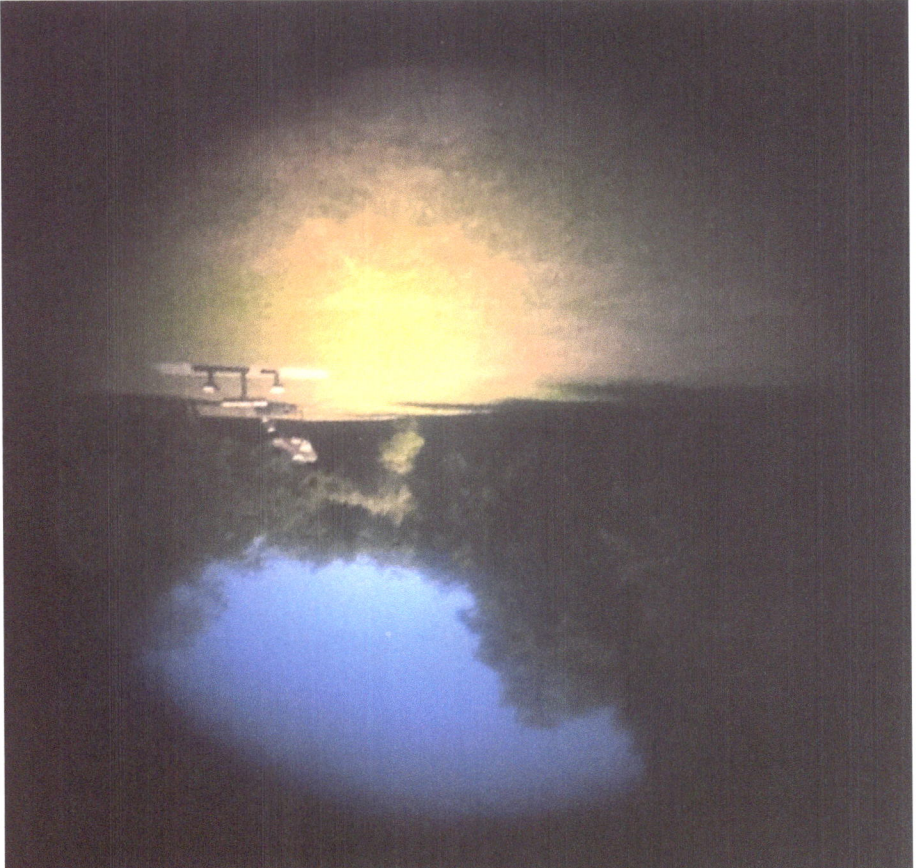

8

Earthly Obscura

Megan Treasure

Megan Treasure is an environmental sculptor, installation artist, and ceramicist.

Her work is grounded, contemplative, feminine, tactually enticing, and often includes the observer in the work by inviting an interaction to take place. Ecology and art education began early for Megan and have continued to form strong bonds in her work.

This is an ephemeral earthen-sculpture that incorporates a "camera obscura". The sculpture allows for people to look inside and view the *inverse*-image that is projected; "As Above, So Below".

The focus of my work over the past few years has been both permanent and temporary structures built as catalysts for experiences with nature. Visitors are often encouraged to engage with the sculptures from the inside out, contemplating the exterior from within. It is always interesting for me to see how individuals interact with a piece; each person adds a 'layer' to the artwork.

I enjoy the transitions, alterations, and the ways people and the environment manipulate the art. I encourage people to photograph, film, draw or write about their interaction with the sculpture and share it with me.

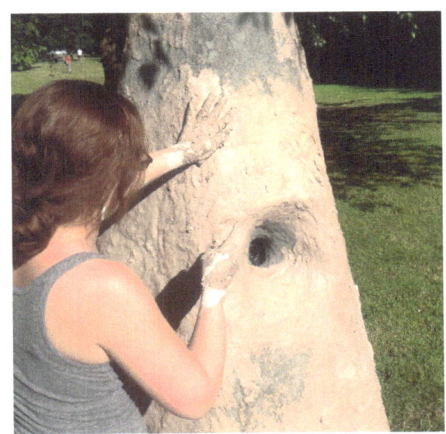

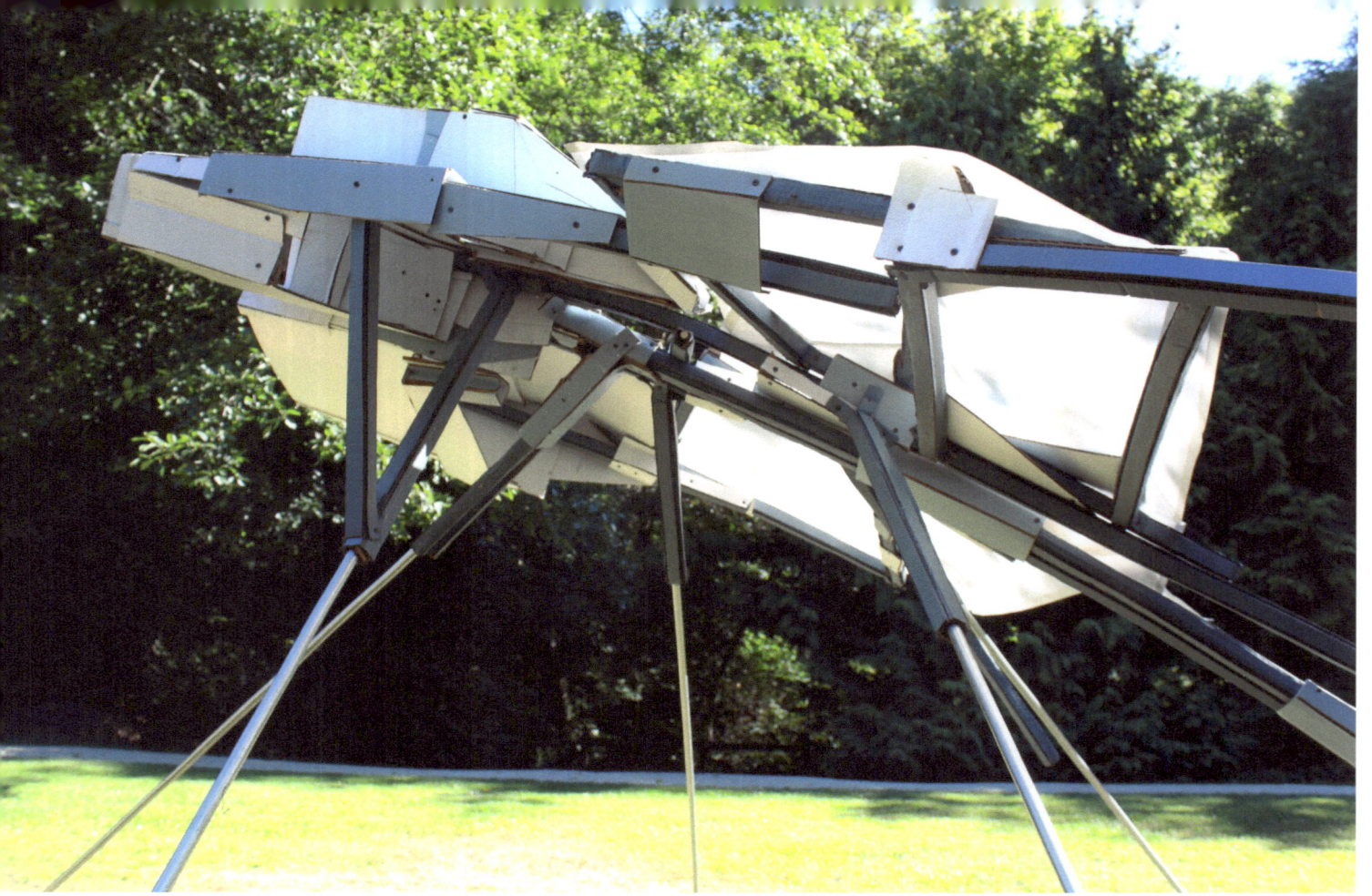

My work revolves around text and structure. I am interested in how language can add life to an object or space, by implying a human presence. I am equally interested in how the structure of the support for that text can affect that voice.

In combining these elements, I find the beginnings of a narrative, and allow the viewer to take it where it might go.

My materials and methods of construction are obvious and common. I prefer to use cardboard, house paint, drywall screws and tape – normal stuff, things we all know well. I intend for the work to have to struggle to keep itself up. I relate to that. I understand that it is frequently not built to last. I also relate to that.

Typically, the text appears to be the most concrete element, while

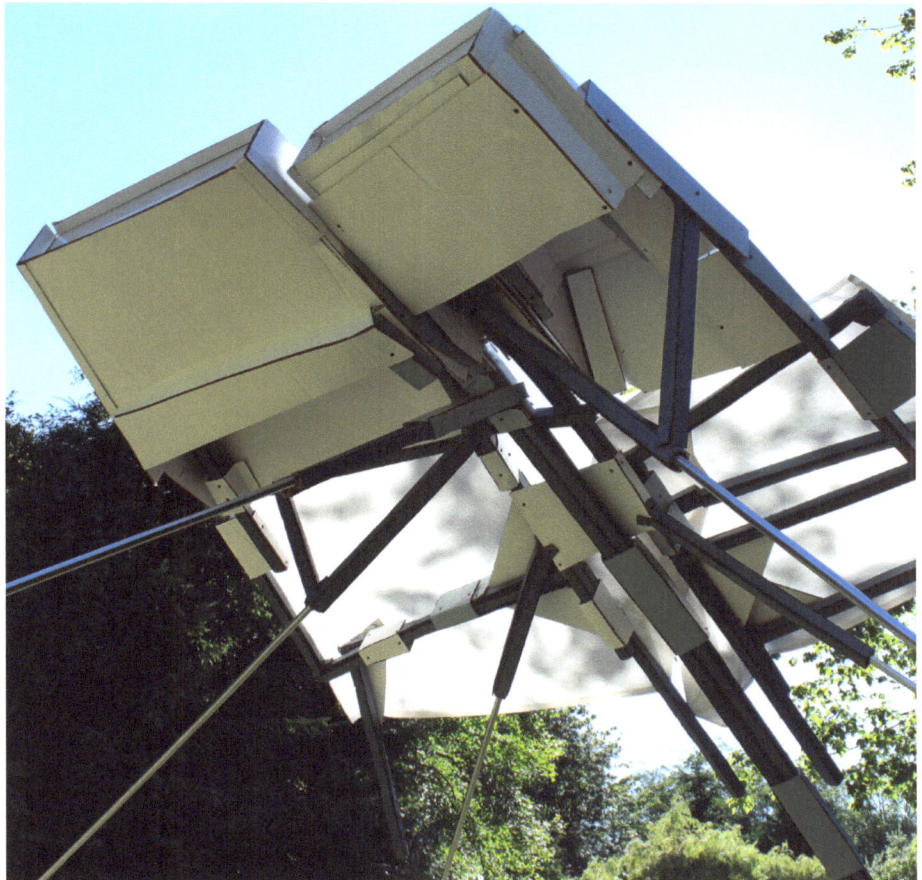

9

Glider

Tom Hughes

the structure is usually haphazard. In human terms, the words are the mind in association to the constructed body, and the bodies I build are often visibly awkward and unstable. In truth, all of it is unstable.

The works are energetically, emphatically built, more by instinct than by intellect. They have more to do with feelings than physics. And so ultimately they suffer:

they bend and collapse. They give way, echoing us.

The essence of the work circles around play, loss, instability, uncertainty, mortality, and absurdity.

These are heavy ideas, but they are still light pieces. The light usually overshadows the weight, but it's there, buried deep.

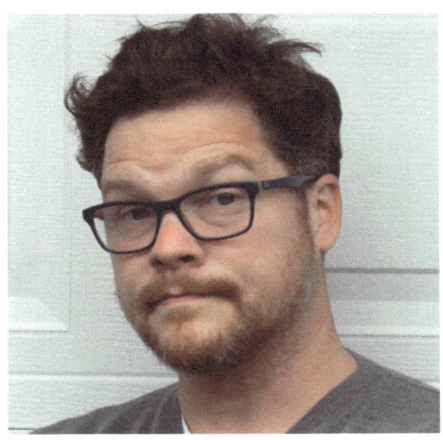

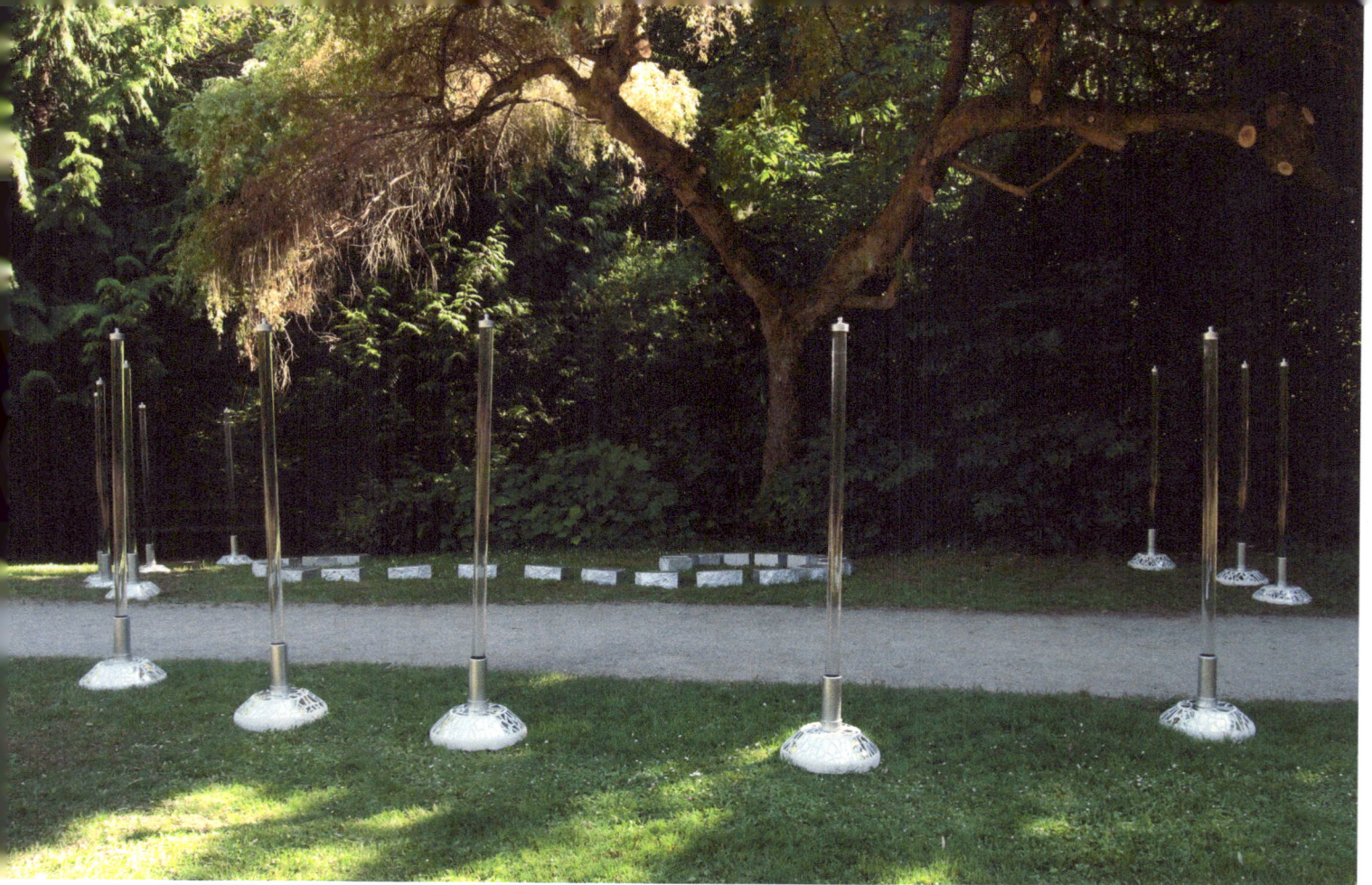

Willow Water manifests an invisible segment of the arboreal hydraulic cycle.

A veil of prismatic, water-filled columns, shimmering with shattered mirrors, maps the dripline of this magnificent Weeping Willow. Such a tree performs many essential services within the riverbank ecosystem, and her gnarled branches and leafy canopy create a living sanctuary.

Sadly, this remarkable beauty was scheduled to be cut down for fear that these long arching branches might be unsafe.

Through the process of curating and creating this installation, the groundskeepers became convinced to prune the limbs severely, rather than destroy this benevolent sentient being,

The sculptural columns are placed to trace the underground rootlets that would have mirrored the tips of the branches at the dripline: as above, so below.

The pathway of silvery stones is inscribed with this reflective poem:

Deanna Pindell

http://www.deannapindell.net

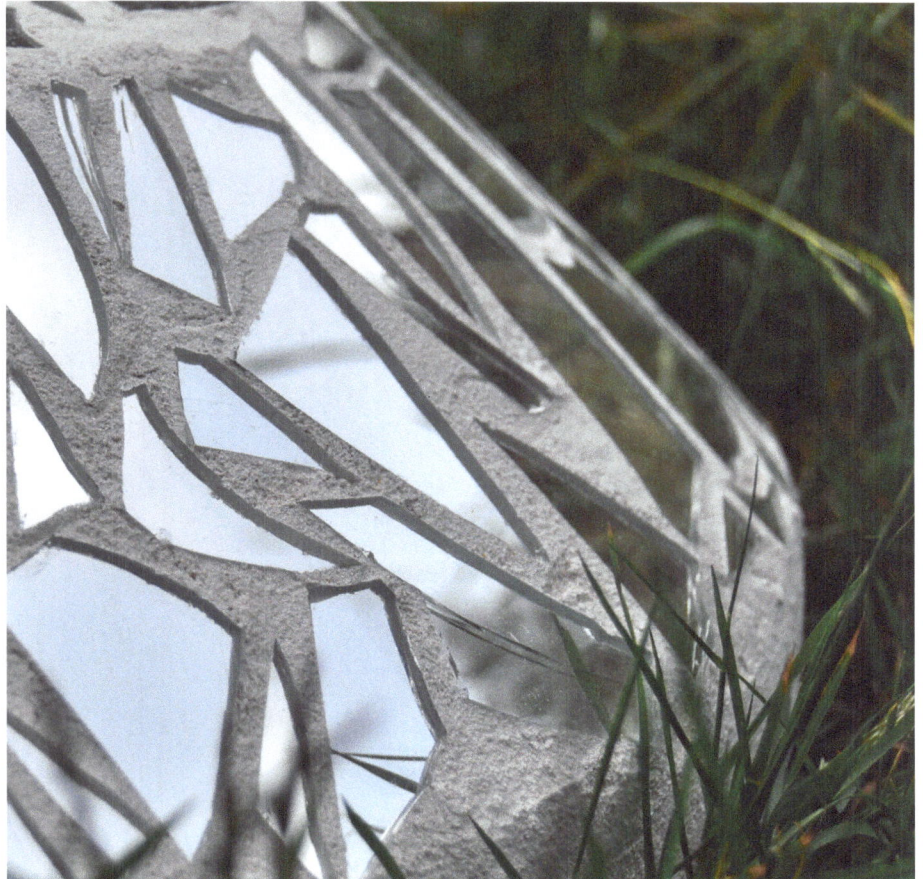

Willow Water

Deanna Pindell

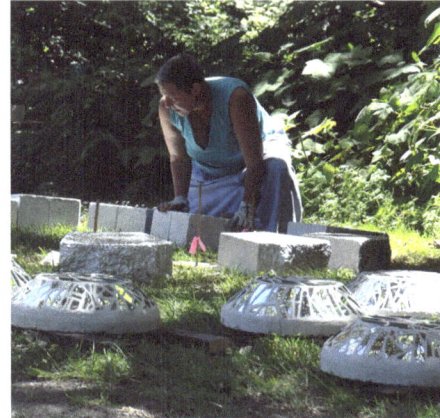

In water we evolved
Of water we are made
From water we are born
With water we live
To water we return
By water we may know

- David Haley,
from *the future
and other creations*

Water quality, deforestation, habitat, climate change: Deanna Pindell seeks positive, functional solutions to these complex and entangled issues through her sculpture, installation, performative conversations and public art. *"We All Share the Same Water"* is perhaps her best-known Eco-artwork, a storm-water remediation intervention in a public park in North Carolina. Another exten-sive project is *"The Soil Remembers"*, a playful trail of discovery designed for Fort Worden State Park (WA, USA) in collaboration with a team of artists and soils scientists; this project integrated art, science exploration and education, a Microbe Manifesto, seven locations across 400 acres, and included an ongoing website:
http://www.soilremembers.com

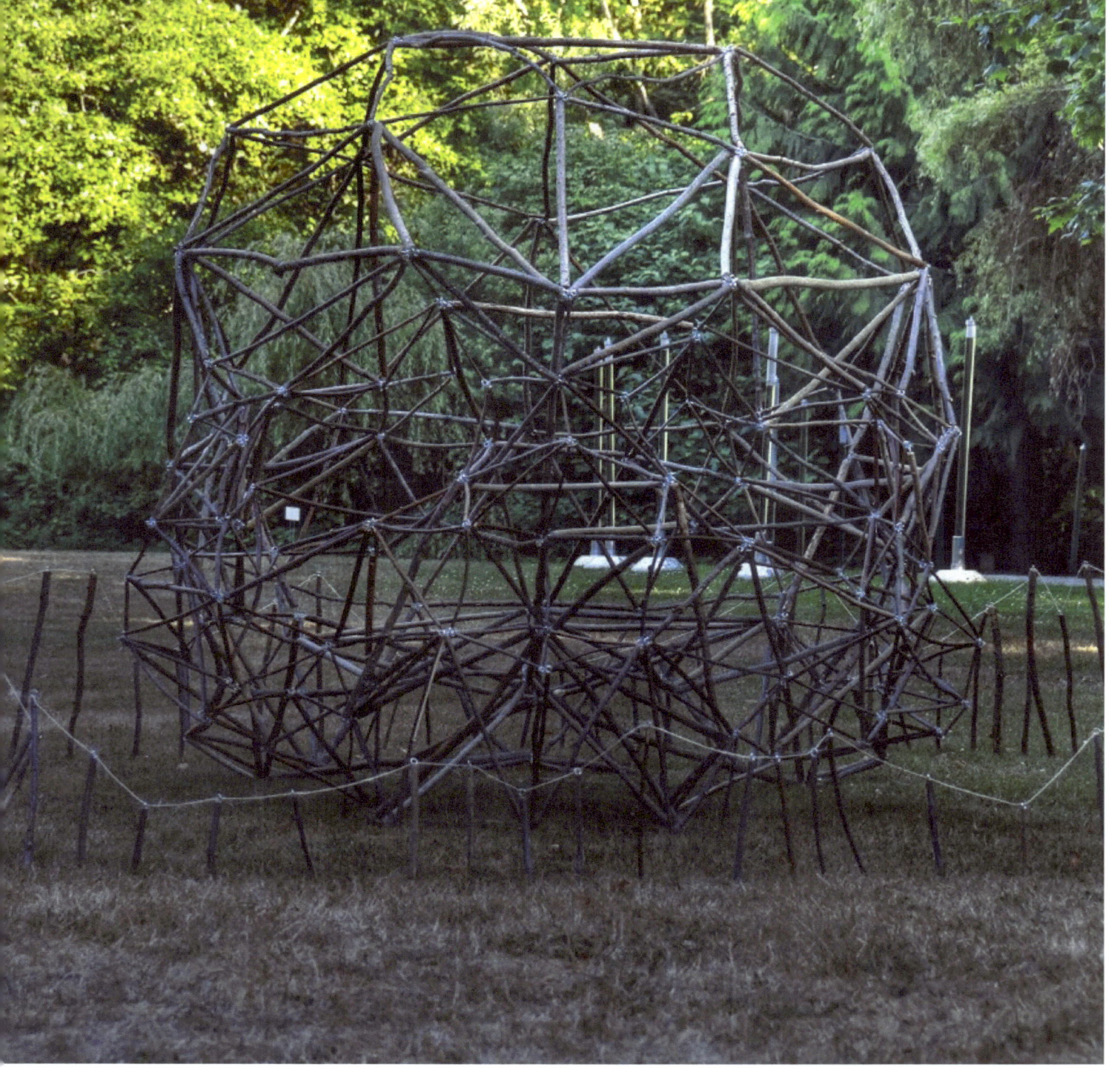

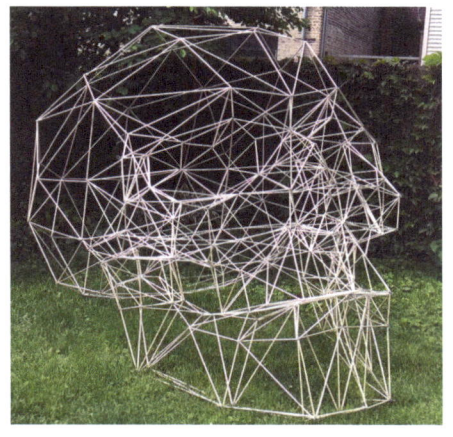

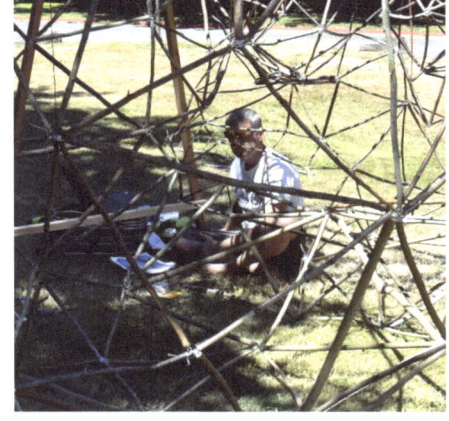

Crania Geodesica: Carkeek
Joshua Harker

This 8 foot geodesic skull is a new work & created onsite from sticks collected from the area. I have become known for my work with skulls as part of my subject matter. This sculpture is based on a geodesic design I created & used to build a similar piece in late 2013 for Dia de los Muertos/La Calaca festival in Mexico. That piece was part of a video projection mapping installation & had a fully enclosed surface. This piece consists of only the framed edges & allows it to be seen through. The framework skull symbolizes our physical state of being and impermanence in the ever changing world. It stands as a testament to the human experience while the surrounding universe flows through it, existing wherein physical and spiritual states meet on a perpetual crossroads to briefly exist as one. I specifically wanted to use materials collected from the area for construction as to further support the metaphor that the organized manifestation of the piece comes from & belongs to the environment that it exists in.

I like to use the skull as a stock subject given that it is so absolutely universally recognized & revered. The varying interpretations across cultures & time allow so much room for me to play artistically. I personally find beauty in the strength & character of the form but also in it as a symbol of impermanence & transition. I find the juxtaposition of the obvious dark connotations associated with it because of death interesting in that it speaks to our fears of the unknown & our certain personal demise. I can think of no more powerful of an image or form in regards to the human psyche other than that of a mother. I see the concept of heaven as an attempt to pair the motherly comfort of love & the terrifying unknown of death into a psychologically manageable "afterlife". Quite the pair… life & death.

Joshua Harker (b.1970) is an American artist considered a pioneer & visionary in 3D printed art & sculpture. His series of "unmakeable" technically complex tangles is credited as the first to break the design & manufacturing threshold of possibility. He has expanded his incorporation of digital tools & technology to further bridge with traditional mediums in regards to concept, design, & construction. Declared a prodigy as a young child, he assumed the identity of an artist from his earliest pursuits. His parents were both artists connected to Grant Wood through his colleague & former student John Bloom & his wife Isabel. Joshua's young life included post 60's off-grid communal living, Hell's Angels babysitters, complete artistic immersion, and family tragedy. Joshua has attended the Kansas City Art Institute and St. Ambrose University as well as later studying anatomy & forensic arts. Joshua's fascination with digital sculpture and 3 dimensional printing technology began as a commercial sculptor and designer in the toy, invention and design, special effects, and product development industries.

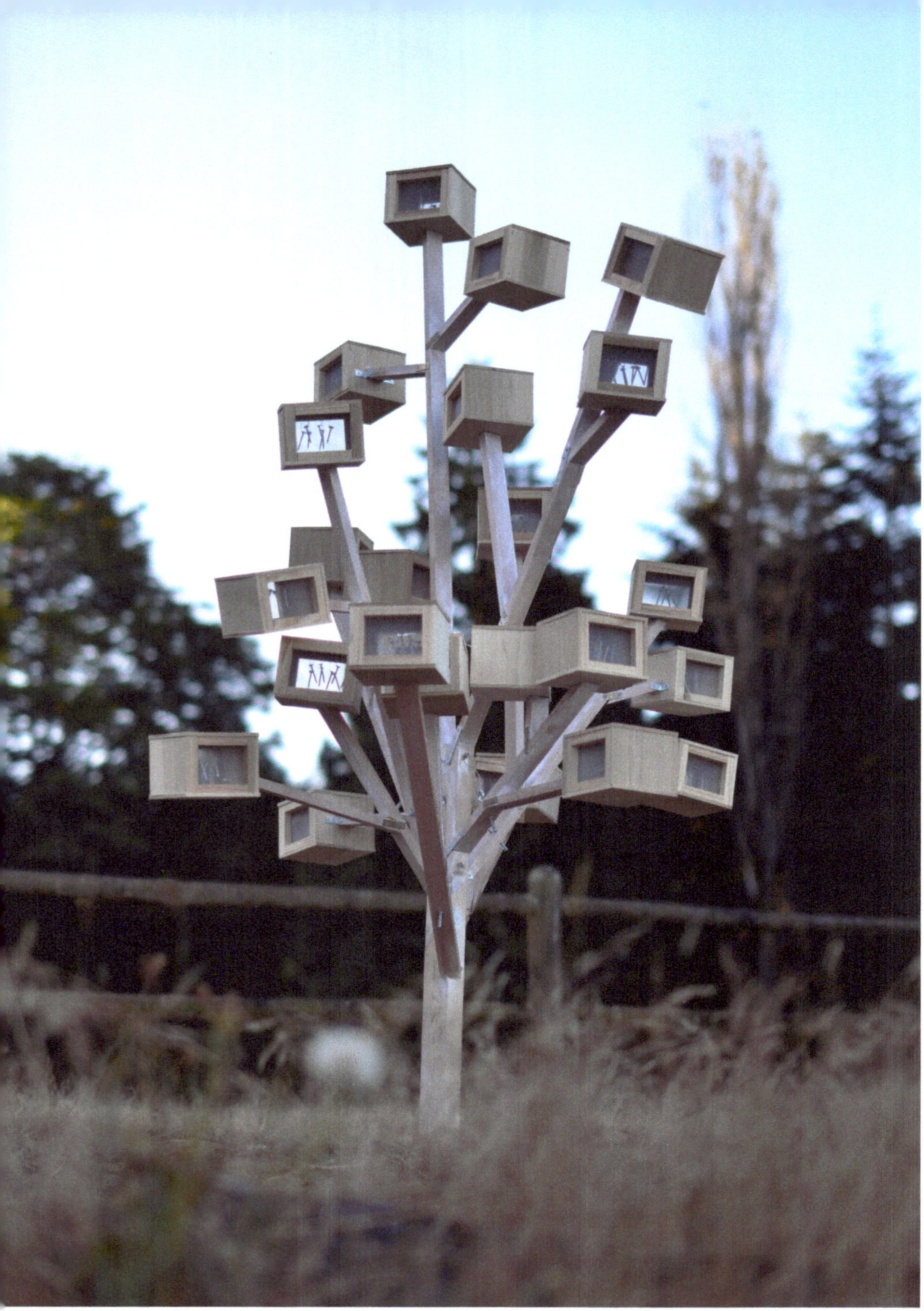

Sound Tree is a sound sculpture, the *Sound,* a reference this and to its temporary home on the shore of Puget Sound. The concept arose from my previous work on an installation using aluminum roofing nails. I was struck with the delicate tinkling sound they make when they come together. It is a silvery cadence, like a wind chime—a sound which belongs to summer.

The initial design phase for this project was a 3D model and print to help me work out the geometry before heading into the wood shop. *Sound Tree* is constructed from Northwest fir and resembles a fig tree in structure. Each branch supporting a wooden box with two mesh sides and nails suspended on thread within. The boxes are oriented in different directions so that as airmass moves through the sculpture, it produces a susurration, much like it does when traveling through a grove of bamboo or a large tree.

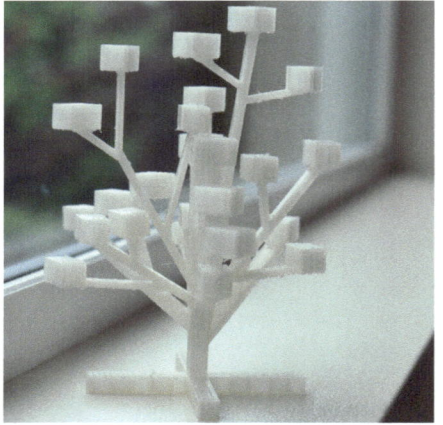

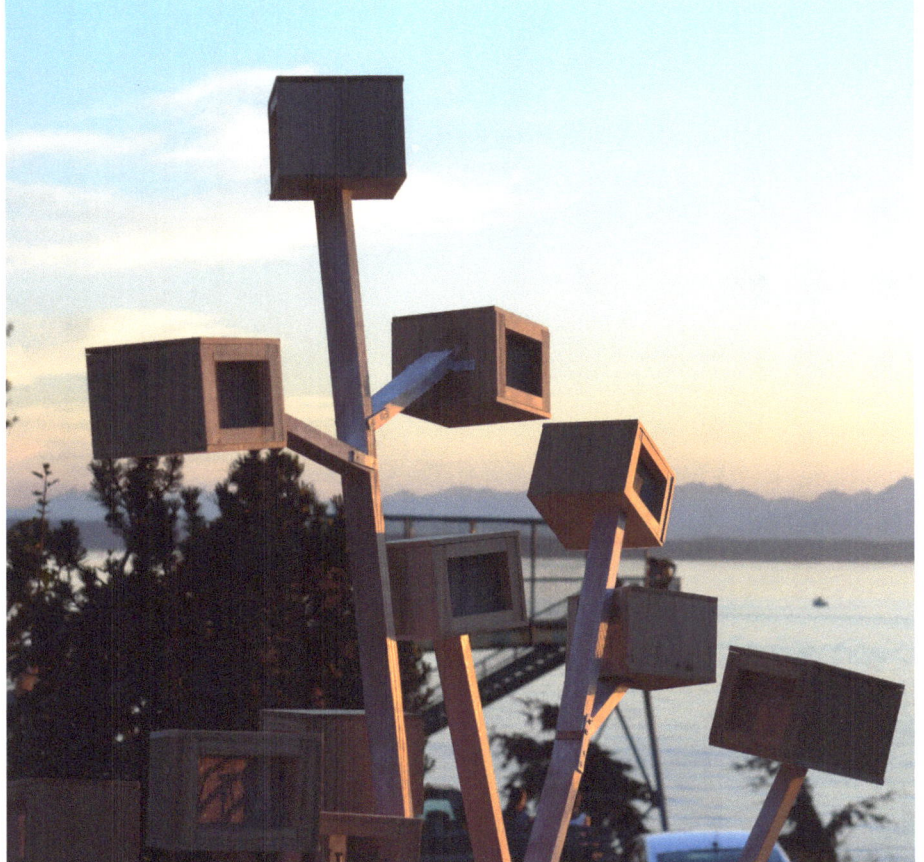

12

Sound Tree

Savina Mason

Savina Mason is a Seattle-based artist working mainly in encaustic. An editor at heart, her work is often focused on finding the bare minimum of elements needed to give an idea visual form. As she constantly experiments, her palette of technique, color, and materials is broad, and changes greatly with each project. Love for order and finding pattern underpins much her work, and conception of landform, observed and imagined, is a recurring theme.

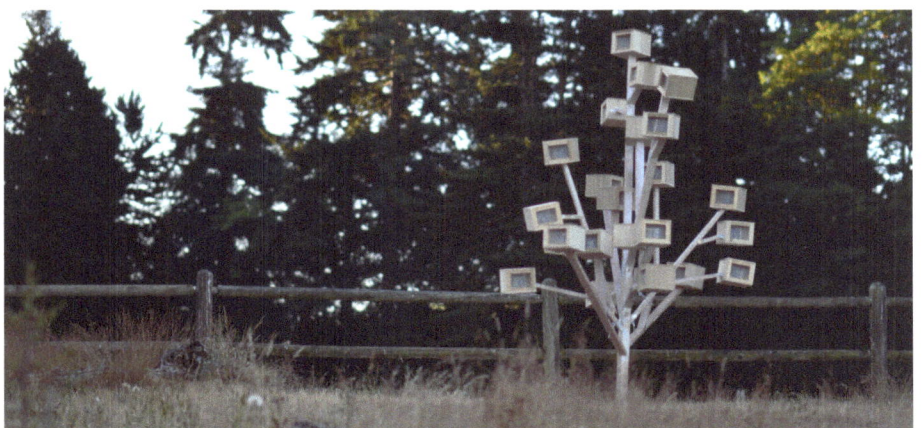

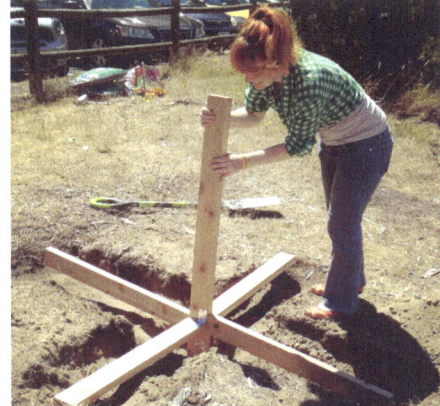

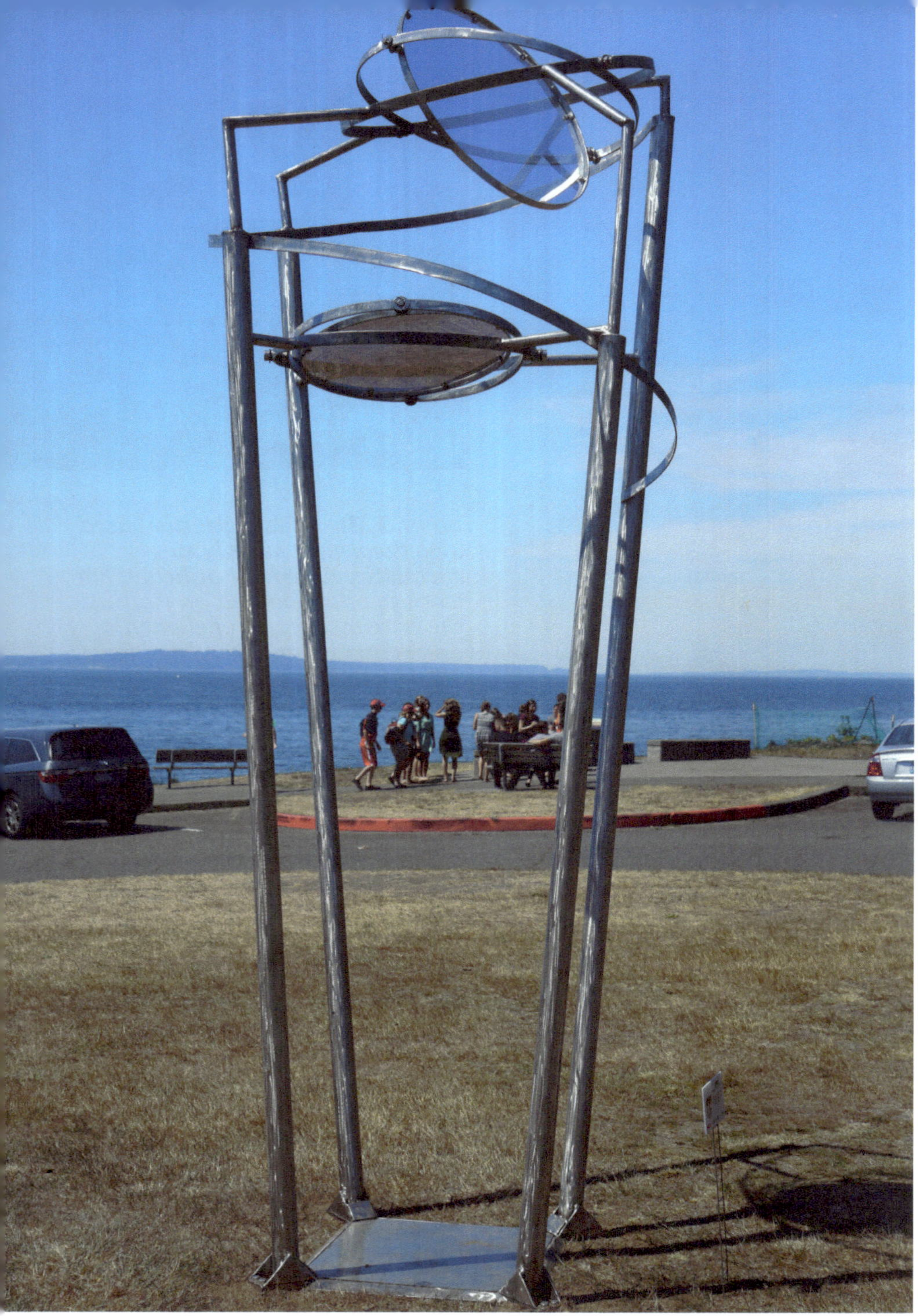

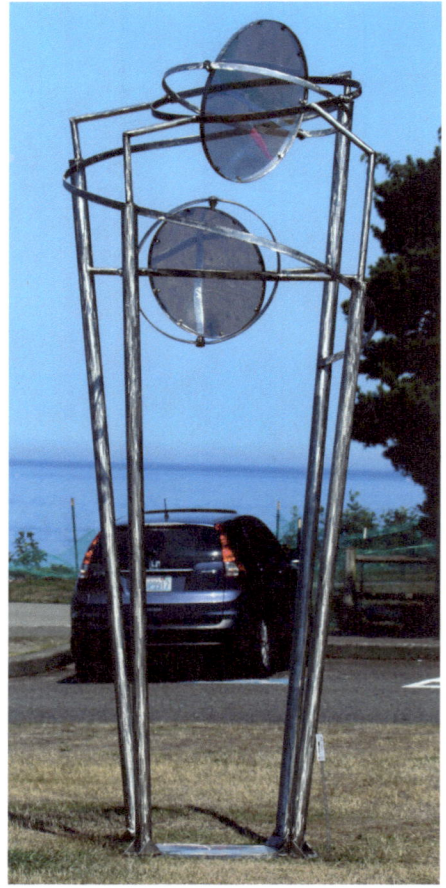

Ken Turner   http://www.kenturner-art.com

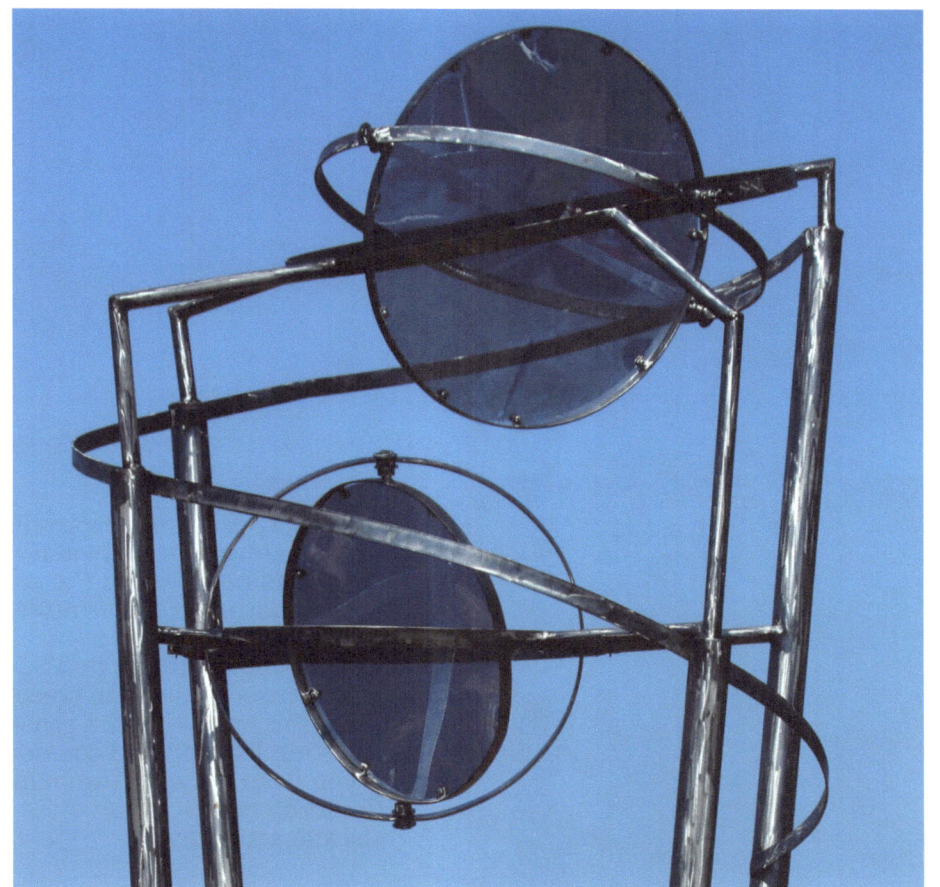

13

Projections and Reflections on the Moment
Ken Turner

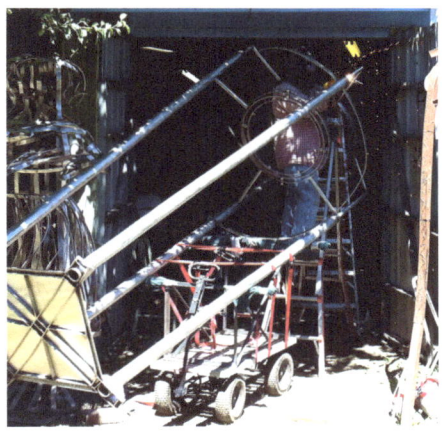

Projections and Reflections on the Moment reflects different aspects of the local environment from moment to moment as it projects images to the heavens. Using semi-transparent mirrors mounted on gimbals the sculpture gives the viewer unaccustomed views of the park, the sky, the water, and perhaps themselves. Whether the mirrors are rotating or not the images will change with the light and time providing a fresh perspective.

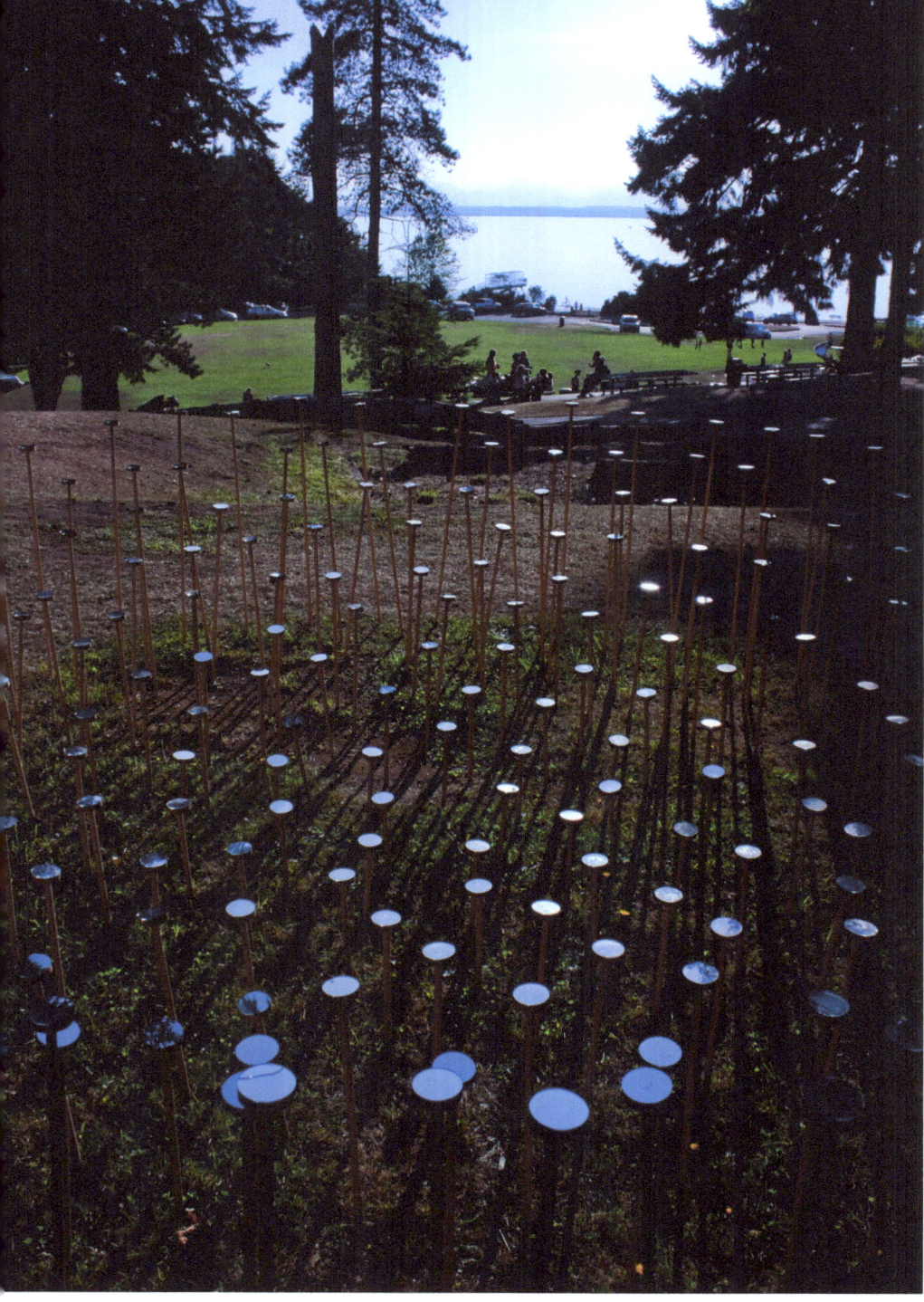

"Sky Feeder" draws its inspiration from the interaction between humans and nature, and the self-discovery nature often arouses, to create a new take on a reflecting pool. Peer in and see yourself, the sky, and the trees above interlaced with the grass below, then look up and consider how you interact with the many different elements in the landscape around you.

"Sky Feeder" is a physical mantra, combining repetition and simple materials: 238 wood-backed mirrors mounted atop wood dowels laid out in concentric rings to form a 12 foot circular sculpture. The final installation process involved a dozen volunteers (major thanks!) who helped place each dowel by hand. The mirrors step down toward the center to create a parabolic bowl that gathers in the sky. Unfinished wood elements will weather naturally during the exhibit, evolving from their own time in nature.

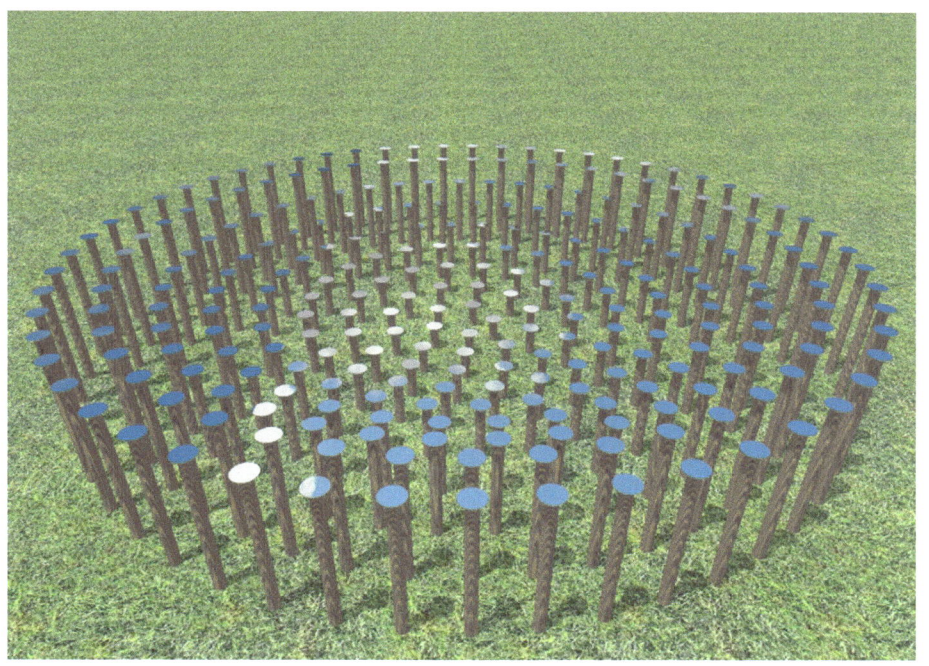

Sky Feeder

Teresa Stern

Teresa Stern is a Seattle artist who lives in the north 'hood of Ballard. She has a background in architecture and design, and has been painting since high school. She is also committed to environmental sustainability, both personally and as an artist. Her work often includes elements of or references to both the natural and the built environment.

Teresa works in oils and mixed media installations. Her paintings explore ecology and landscapes, while her installation work has to date focused on interactions with nature. Teresa has studied painting and drawing at the Pratt Fine Arts Center and Gage Academy of Art in Seattle, as well as art and art history as part of architecture studies at the Universities of Illinois and Arizona.

Teresa has had several exhibits of her work, including solo shows at SPACE and Shelton City Hall, and group shows at Allied Arts of Yakima Valley, and Art on the Ridge in the NW and at Hadley Hotel Studios in North Carolina.

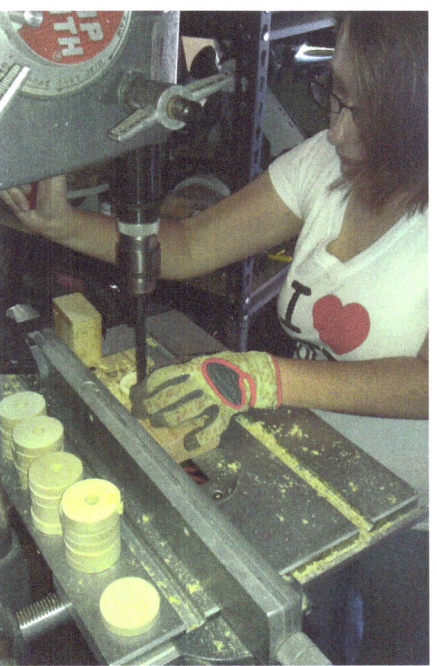

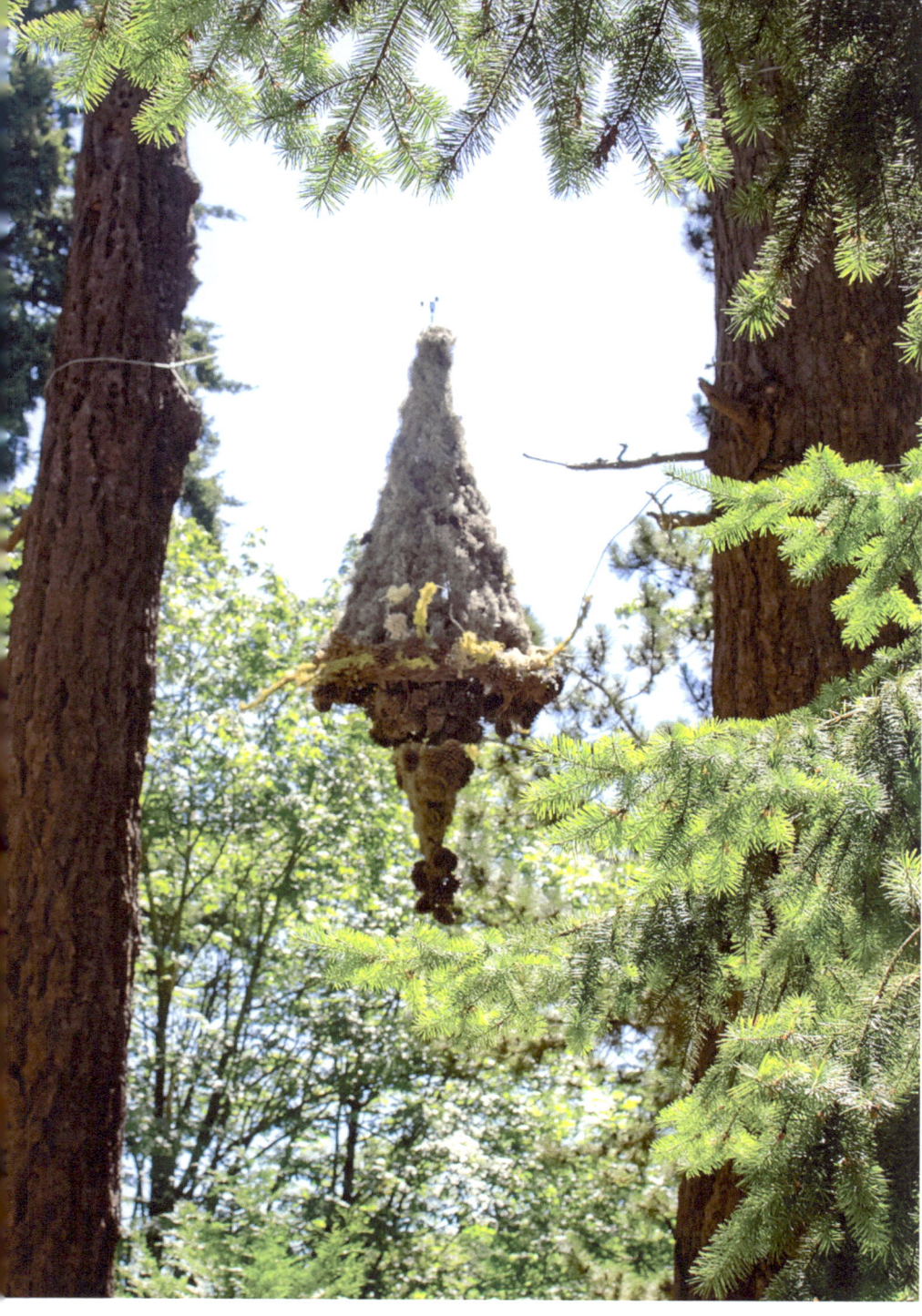

Tree of Life inhabits the space in between; balancing amidst the earth and in the sky, and transitioning along with the weather and seasons. She is supported by the tree stumps yet alone and unguarded in the elements. To watch her twist in the wind can be mesmerizing. Looking straight up feels unnatural; we feel unbalanced, and extra attention to stabilizing our footing on the earth is needed. She hangs in the unknown. Will some portions of her survive and thrive while others decay? Will birds use her to nest, or will she be picked apart by curious visitors? She represents maintaining stability and balance in the unknown; just as we face our own personal or planetary futures. Made from natural materials: branches, moss, seed heads, pine cones and grasses, Terra is infused with the same spirit as forest nurse-log, created with living plants and bird seed in the hope that she will serve as a source of shelter and nourishment to animals. She was inspired by the jellyfish illustrations of Ernst Haeckel.

Terra Holcomb   http://www.terraholcomb.com

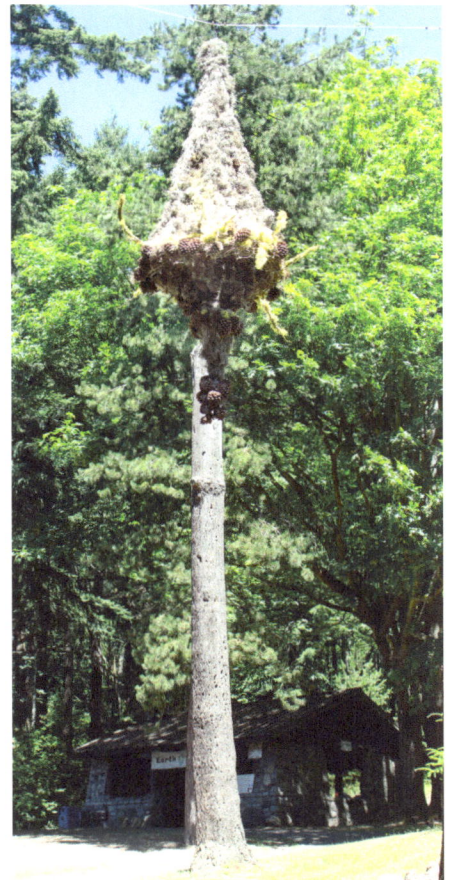

15

Tree of Life

Terra Holcomb

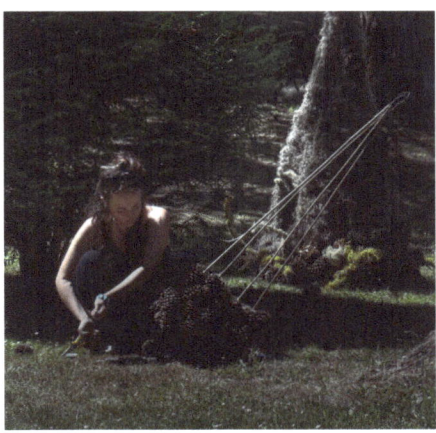

I was born on Earth Day and my parents decided to name me Terra. Fittingly, my work is inspired and created in the wilderness. I routinely use natural materials to create dresses, sets, installations, mandalas and now chandeliers. My need to create in solitude means that I frequently travel in the Pacific Northwest on my own. By doing so, I am able to quietly respond to my environment and work quickly without disruption. The stillness of my trips is a form of meditation and spirituality. I feel most alive when I am surrounded by the ocean, desert or rainforest.

I recently taught a workshop at the Seattle Art Museum Sculpture park for Earth day and have another event planned there in August. Engaging the public with art and natural materials was deeply moving and inspirational for all involved.

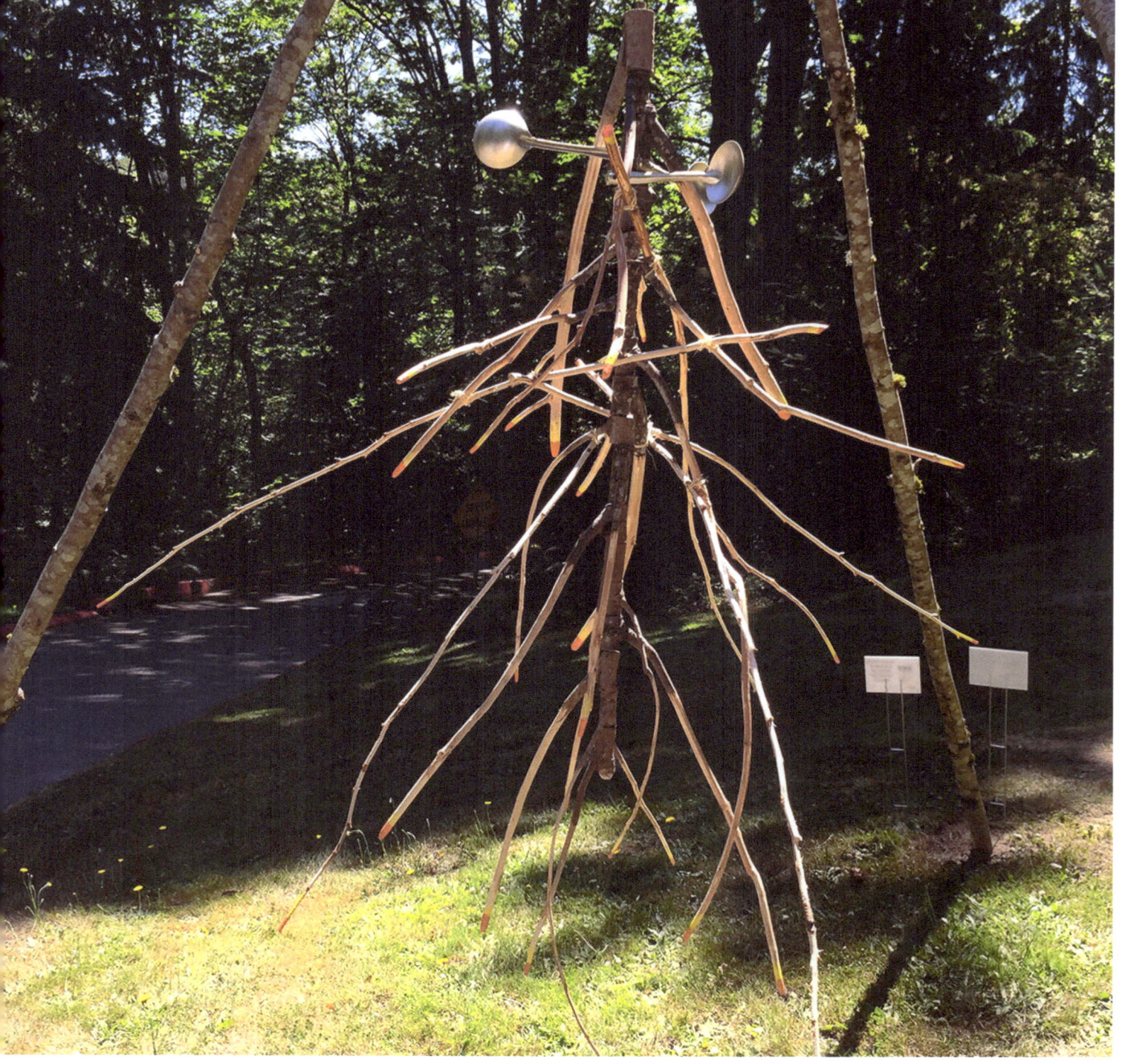

　　　　　　　　Fred Lisaius　　　　　　　　http://www.fredlisaius.com

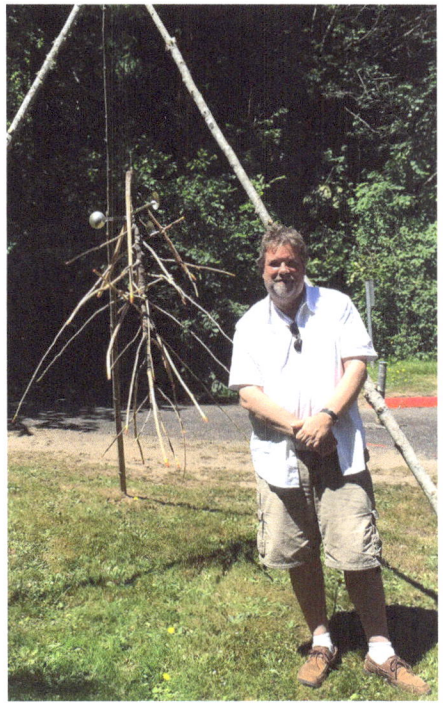

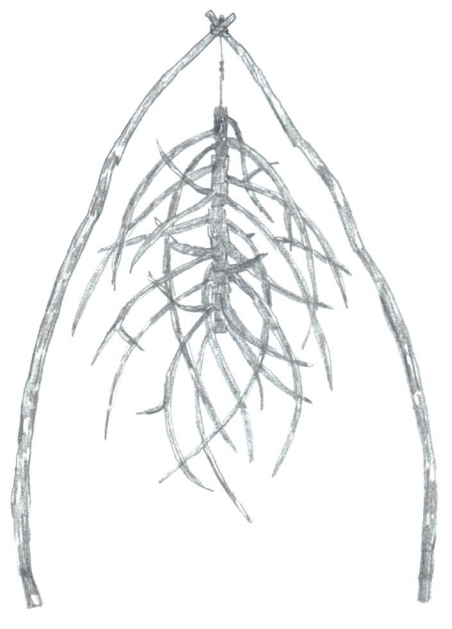

16

Slow Dance

Fred Lisaius

Fred Lisaius earned a B.F.A. with honors from the Rhode Island School of Design. He is represented by art galleries around the United States and is included in many private and corporate collections, including the Mayo Clinic, Nordstrom, Amazon, Park Nicolette Clinic, Swedish Hospital, Ex Officio, and many others.

"My work is often inspired by nature and includes themes of community, tolerance, diversity, leadership, and change." Fred gives back to the community whenever possible by teaching art to "at risk" teens, donating artworks to auctions, and being a juror for exhibitions.

Branches extending from the trunk of a tree arc, twist and bend in a quest for light. It is a beautiful slow dance that echoes the challenges in our own lives and can be made more apparent through sculpture.

I propose a sculpture made from tree branches that hangs from a large tree branch. It will be fitted with a swivel that will allow it to gently rotate in the breeze. It will feel like a dance.
The deeper Fred goes into the forest the closer he feels to the truth. Off of the trail, there is a quiet calm where ideas can be contemplated and refined. In his paintings, Fred utilizes the forum of nature to explore our relation-

ship to the natural world and to each other.

When it's foggy outside, Fred sees everything more clearly. Shapes are simplified, colors subdued and a veil of mystery is cast. He likes to incorporate transitions in his paintings- spaces such as change of season, day into night and awake to sleep are realms where the imagination and reality coexist.

Nature is a mirror that we can look into and understand ourselves better. Fred's paintings provide a portal to a place where dramas unfold, explorations can occur and discoveries are made.

Books and Catalogs

Exhibition Catalogs:

Heaven and Earth
Outdoor Sculpture Exhibition at Carkeek Park

2009 Annual Exhibition
Juried by Jess Nostrand

Across the Divide
Contemporary Art from the Scablands

2009 East|West
Emerging Artist Exchange

Kate Vrijmoet
Essential Gestures

Across the Divide II
Art from Big Sky Country

Gideon: Becoming
A story of Love and Cosmology

Resident Alien
Local Artists from Europe and Beyond

CoCA Parks 2010
Outdoor Sculpture Exhibitions
at Carkeek Park and Cougar Mountain Park

2010 Annual Exhibition
Memory Upgrade: Juried by Juan Alonso

Heaven and Earth III:
Cycles of Return
Outdoor Sculpture Exhibition at Carkeek Park

Limb from Limb
The Arboreal Art of Peppé

(Un)Sanctioned
13 Contemporary Urban Artists

2011 Annual Exhibition
Juried by Gary Hill

Heaven and Earth IV: Rootbound
Outdoor Art Exhibition at Carkeek Park

Across the Divide IV
The New Boondooks

Show Us Yours
2012 CoCA Members' Show

Alive, Dead
28 Artists' Interpretations

2012 Annual Exhibition
Juried by MK Guth

Whitewashed
Joseph Gregory Rossano

CoCA Collision
Past, Present, & Future
CoCA Members' Show, 2013

Heaven and Earth 5
Acclimatized
Outdoor Art Exhibition at Carkeek Park

Ceci N'est Pas Une Pipe
Flameworking on the Brink of Legalization

Who Are You?
2014 CoCA Members' Show

2014 Annual Exhibition
PostGlamism: Glam Art in the 21st Century
Juried by Michael Sweney

Monographs:

Otherwise This Stone
Poetry by David Francis

Field Notes from the Chimalapa Wilderness
David Francis, Oaxaca, 2000-2012

The Stars are Made from Love & Beauty
Joe Reno Journals

Available at CoCA Gallery and:

www.lulu.com/spotlight/cocaseattle

In 2009, CoCA initiated this publication series as part of our ongoing campaign to expand our activities outside of the conventional gallery space and into the public realm.

These books make the exhibitions that we put on in our Georgetown, Gallery and elsewhere accessible to a larger audience over a longer period of time than the lifetime of the actual show, and in a more physical, tactile form than the images on our website.

These are high-quality books, printed on demand for us by lulu Publishing, and ordered directly from them.

www.ingramcontent.com/pod-product-compliance
Lightning Source LLC
Chambersburg PA
CBHW040748200526
45159CB00023B/1771